BLOODY BRITISH HISTORY
HISTORY
PETERBOROUGH

T0333463

BLOODY BRITISH HISTORY

HISTORY

PETERBOROUGH

JEAN HOOPER

The
History
Press

Fist pubished 2012
Reprinted 2022

The History Press
97 St George's Place,
Cheltenham, Gloucestershire, GL50 3QB
www.thehistorypress.co.uk

British Library Cataloguing in Publication Data.
A catalogue record for this book is available from the British Library.

ISBN 978 0 7524 8271 2

Typesetting and origination by The History Press
Printed iby TJ Books Limited, Padstow, Cornwall

CONTENTS

INTRODUCTION

Let's take a step back 150 years from today's city, dominated by cathedral and church, with the pedestrianised centre, shopping centres, leisure facilities, modern townships and open countryside surrounding the old heart of the town.

The market place is in front of the cathedral gates and the old, narrow streets leading off the market square are busy with little shops and breweries; horse-drawn vehicles and the occasional sedan chair move around goods and people. The new railway is changing the town and the immediate outskirts as rail companies bring industrial works and rows of company-built terraced houses stretching out into the countryside.

Three hundred years earlier, and although the cathedral is unaltered, the great abbey of St Peter and its buildings have mostly been destroyed by Henry VIII.

Eight hundred years ago and the Burgh of St Peter is still overlooked by the same church, though the houses of the town lie behind the abbey, not in front of it. The earlier name of the town, Burgh, came about when a wall was built round the monastery area. The wealth of that monastery and its lands led to the name Gildenburgh, the golden town.

Over 1,300 years ago and the local royal ruler has begun to build a Christian monastery close to a small settlement known as Medeshamstede, the homestead by the meadows. The rise of Peterborough has begun, and turbulent and violent times lie ahead for its inhabitants.

PREHISTORY

THE ORIGINS OF PETERBOROUGH

Home to Britain's First Murder Victim?

RICH DEPOSITS OF fossils have come to light in the brick quarries around the town: remains of ichthyosaurs, plesiosaurs, pliosaurs and other marine creatures, some of which can be seen in Peterborough Museum. Belemnites were rather like modern-day squid and formed part of the diet of ichthyosaurs. The hard shells of belemnites could not be digested, so were regurgitated from the stomachs of their predators. A few years ago, a large amount of fossilized belemnites found in a Peterborough clay pit allowed scientists to prove that they had once formed the meal of a 'fish lizard' over 150-160 million years ago. The indigestible parts of the meal were ejected from the ichthyosaur's stomach, leaving behind a pile of prehistoric vomit.

Gravel pits have revealed the bones of other giant creatures that lived in the area after the Age of Dinosaurs such as woolly mammoths, woolly rhinoceros and bears,

Prehistoric seas, and the creatures living in and around them, laid the foundations of the landscape of Peterborough and its surroundings.

Millions of years after the seas had gone, the flat, marshy land areas combined with the slowly rising, more stony country to the west, providing an environment where early man could live and exploit its resources. Thousands of years ago, the ancient forests which covered the area left behind the peat deposits. The fertile black earth was farmed and agriculture became a major source of work and wealth. In more recent times the local brick industry flourished thanks to the presence of Oxford Clay, formed in the Jurassic period. Gravel deposits, formed when ice covered and then retreated from the land, are still being quarried today for local building works.

which would have been hunted by the first humans who lived in this area.

BRITAIN'S EARLIEST KNOWN MURDER VICTIM?

As the Ice Age ended, early man would have hunted animals, caught fish and gathered plants for food, moving around as the seasons changed. Gradually, instead of following their food source, people began to settle here, breeding livestock and planting crops. The pasture land of the Fens, fresh water and slightly higher country to the west provided a perfect place to live and take advantage of the rich resources of the area. As people began to work a piece of land and keep their animals in one place, they perhaps came into conflict with others who were also establishing their claim to use a particular pasture or trackway.

It is impossible to know the reason why, but it is certain that nearly 6,000 years ago a young man living in this area was hit by the arrow that ended his life. Excavations carried out in 1975 at Fengate on the east of the city revealed the skeleton of a man with the flint arrowhead still embedded in his ribs. Did he attempt to protect himself, or did death come too quickly? Nearby were three more groups of bones, belonging to two children and a woman. Did they die violently at the same time, or were they united after death?

Over the years, Fengate and other sites in and around the city have revealed evidence of the earliest inhabitants of this landscape. Bronze-Age field systems, trackways and ditches, and later Iron-Age round houses, clustered together in small groups, show the growth of settlement that eventually developed into our present-day community. Perhaps the most remarkable site to have been discovered can be seen at Flag Fen. A huge wooden platform dating back 3,000 years was probably a ritual site that continued to be used over a long period. A wooden causeway nearly half a mile long led across the marshy land to the artificial island. Bronze- and Iron-Age weapons and jewellery, pottery and even human bones had been carefully placed along one side of the wooden posts.

AD 60

ROMANS

Massacre and Reprisal

THE FIRST EVIDENCE of a Roman presence in the area comes from Longthorpe in Peterborough. A Roman fort big enough to hold half a legion was occupied principally during two periods in the first century AD by soldiers of the famous Legio IX Hispana: the Ninth Legion. The first fortress was built around AD 43 as the Romans moved north and east through Britain, subduing local tribes and protecting their borders. In around AD 61 the area of the fortress was reduced in size following the massacre of most of its soldiers by Boudicca.

Within a few years the IX Legion was moving steadily north, reinforced by soldiers from Germany.

Half a legion could consist of between 2,000 and 3,000 soldiers, so their base would be built somewhere that could support such large numbers. The local countryside was rich in resources with good soil for agriculture, woodland, stone and iron. The fort could easily bring in supplies by land but its proximity to the River Nene and the Fens made transportation by boat an excellent option. Romans later made the first attempts to drain the Fens and the Carr Dyke ran straight to the River Ouse. Developing the Fen Causeway, which linked the 'islands' of drier land in the Fens, also gave them easier access to eastern areas. Ermine Street passed by the legion's base; strategically placed on the edge of what is now East Anglia, this was an ideal location for controlling the frontiers of Roman occupation.

Local people were happy to take advantage of trade with the garrison and settlements soon developed around the outside of a fort. Tradespeople and craftsmen built shops and workshops as well as their homes and before long a sizeable community would be working alongside the Romans. The town of Durobrivae grew up close to the River Nene and spread along Ermine Street. The name Durobrivae means 'fort by the bridge' and a smaller fort would have protected the river crossing there.

Even when the fortress at Longthorpe had been abandoned Durobrivae continued to thrive, its excellent position on lines of communication and plentiful supplies of raw materials meaning that its craftsmen and goods were always in demand. Most of the workshops fronted onto Ermine Street, the great Roman Road which ran from the south to the north of the country. It was one of the biggest industrial sites in Roman Britain producing pottery and metalwork. Locally sourced iron ore was the main metal used but it appears that more valuable metals were also worked here. Although most pottery was made for local use, examples of better quality 'Castor ware' have been found in other parts of Britain and even abroad.

British war chariot.

ROMAN TREASURE!

The wealth and importance of Durobrivae in Roman times are shown by the finds that have been made in the area in modern times. The Water Newton Treasure was found in 1975 and is the earliest Christian silverware found anywhere in the Roman Empire. There were twenty-seven silver items including a jug, cup and bowl engraved with early Christian symbols. There was also a small gold disc. It seems that the treasure had been placed inside a pottery jar and buried in the field outside the town in the fourth century. It is not known why they were hidden. The beautifully engraved objects are now in the British Museum.

ROMAN MASSACRE!

The Iceni occupied lands to the east of this region in an area now covered by Norfolk and part of Suffolk. The Romans sometimes allowed 'client kings' to rule their own people, and this was the case with the Iceni. After their king Prasutagus died he had hoped that the Roman Emperor, Nero, would allow his daughters to rule after him. However, the Romans took complete control of their kingdom and confiscated property belonging to important tribespeople. The furious Iceni were to suffer even greater punishment and humiliation: Prasutagus' widow, Queen Boudicca, was stripped and publically flogged and her daughters raped by the soldiers.

Revenge followed swiftly as Boudicca and her followers inflicted crushing defeats on the mighty Roman army. Gathering together other tribes, Boudicca took advantage of the absence of the governor of Britain and led her warriors to the centres of Roman power in England. First to be attacked was Colchester, where those who had survived the initial onslaught sought refuge in the Temple of Claudius, only to be burned alive as Boudicca destroyed the whole town. The Britons moved on to London and then St Albans, killing the inhabitants and burning the towns. Roman historian Tacitus writes that the IX Legion under the command of Petilius Cerialis went to relieve the siege of Camolodunum (Colchester) but were savagely attacked by Boudicca's army, leaving only the cavalry to escape and flee north again. The sight of Boudicca's army would strike fear into even the most hardened Roman soldier. Before fighting, trumpets would sound and Druids would call upon their gods to bring victory. The heads of captured enemies were displayed on pikes and the screaming warriors, their bodies painted and tattooed, would rush to battle. They were merciless in victory, torturing and mutilating their captives, even women. It is possible that up to 2,000 men of the IX Legion were slaughtered by the Britons before they even reached Camolodunum. This may explain why a smaller fortress was built inside the original defences at Longthorpe, enabling it to be held by fewer soldiers for a short time before the stronghold was abandoned.

A Roman altar, used as the base for a Saxon cross and now in Castor church.

ROMAN PALACE

One of the largest Roman buildings in Britain stood in present-day Castor, overlooking the town of Durobrivae. The massive scale of the building and the quality of the finds associated with it suggest that it was the headquarters and palace of someone of great status in the Roman Empire. Possibly the person who lived here in the mid-third century was a military governor or the governor of an Imperial Estate stretching out from Durobrivae across the Fens. There were certainly high-status villas around the town but they would have been dwarfed by the building on the hill. Extending over 274 metres by 122 metres, the praetorium, or palace, would have dominated the landscape for miles around.

THE FATE OF THE IX LEGION

The fate of the IX Legion has given rise to several theories as to why records ceased to mention their existence. Were soldiers of one of the oldest and most experienced Roman legions wiped out by northern British tribes? Writers and film makers have long been inspired by the enduring mystery of their supposed disappearance from history.

Before being sent to Britain, the IX Legion had fought successfully in Europe and Africa, earning the nickname 'Hispana' after their successes in Spain. As the Roman army moved northwards through Britain, the IX was divided into two forces, one based at Longthorpe, Peterborough, and the other at Newark. Soldiers from Peterborough would have been close enough to march to the rescue of towns targeted by Boudicca. They were unable to withstand the attack by the 'Warrior Queen' and her fearsome British tribesmen and had to retreat to their base after suffering huge losses. Up to 2,000 men may have died and reinforcements were sent from Germany to take their place. The IX Legion moved north again, basing themselves at Lincoln, and then York, where the last evidence of them comes from AD 117.

Were they sent to fight against the Caledonians, who slaughtered the whole legion? Or were they simply sent overseas, before or after fighting along the border country? Some members of the 'Hispana' at least seem to have been in Europe and Africa again after AD 120 – were they just the survivors of an earlier massacre? Certainly the IX Legion is no longer in existence in a later list of all Roman legions and no mention of its fate is recorded...

THE DEATH OF BOUDICCA

Boudicca must have been a strong and ruthless leader. After her routing of the IX Legion, Roman historians were at pains to emphasize her wild, barbaric appearance and describe her as a terrifying woman, tall, with long red hair and clothed in the bright colours and jewellery of a Celtic chieftain. The Druids that accompanied her army called down curses on her enemies, who faced torture and certain death at her hands. Following the carnage at Colchester, London and St Albans, the Romans gathered their forces against the British warriors. Boudicca's army was beaten and legend says that she took poison to avoid capture. It is not known where the final battle took place but a legend places Boudicca's burial in a site now underneath King's Cross Station in London.

AD 500

THE SAXONS

Founder of Monastery Dies in Mysterious Circumstances!

THE SAXONS WERE a Germanic tribe who possibly first arrived in this country as raiders or mercenaries in the fifth century. By the time the story of Medeshampstede begins they were living throughout England, with farms and small settlements in this area. Two of the major Saxon kingdoms were Mercia and Northumbria, and both were connected to the monastery by the side of the River Nene.

In the seventh century the Saxon kingdom of Mercia roughly covered the area of the Midlands today. It was ruled by Penda, a pagan king, and the area around Medeshamstede was ruled by his son Peada, king of the Middle Angles. Probably as part of an attempt to broker

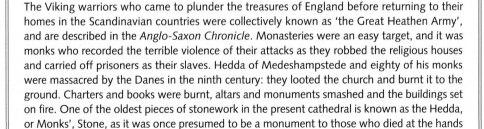

The Viking warriors who came to plunder the treasures of England before returning to their homes in the Scandinavian countries were collectively known as 'the Great Heathen Army', and are described in the *Anglo-Saxon Chronicle*. Monasteries were an easy target, and it was monks who recorded the terrible violence of their attacks as they robbed the religious houses and carried off prisoners as their slaves. Hedda of Medeshampstede and eighty of his monks were massacred by the Danes in the ninth century: they looted the church and burnt it to the ground. Charters and books were burnt, altars and monuments smashed and the buildings set on fire. One of the oldest pieces of stonework in the present cathedral is known as the Hedda, or Monks', Stone, as it was once presumed to be a monument to those who died at the hands of the Danes.

It was mainly the Danes who raided the eastern coast of England but, like the Saxons before them, they gradually began to settle here permanently. By the early part of the eleventh century, the Danish king Canute (Knut) claimed to be 'king of all the English'.

Contemporary image of an Anglo-Saxon king in his armour.

some sort of peace between Mercia and the Christian kingdom of Northumbria, marriages were arranged between children of their respective kings.

Peada was married to Alflaed, King Oswiu of Northumbria's daughter, with the condition that he become a Christian. He and his wife returned to Medeshamstede with four monks and set about establishing a monastery. Whether peace between the kingdoms had ever really been intended, Peada's father was killed in battle by his wife's father soon after the return to Medeshamstede. Although Peada was allowed to continue as king of the Middle Angles, Bede says that he was betrayed and murdered by his own wife, poisoned at the time of the Easter feasts – presumably being celebrated at the new monastery.

Peada's brother Wulfhere became king and fought successfully against the Northumbrians. He ensured the growth of the new monastery with the help of the first abbot, Saxulf. Although praised as a good king who gave lands and wealth to spread Christianity in the area, another legend paints him as the ruthless murderer of his own sons, Wulfade and Rufine. Whilst out hunting, it says, both brothers met the holy St Chad, who baptised them as Christians. Wulfhere was a Pagan and was so angry that his sons had become Christians that he cut off their heads with his sword. He later regretted what he had done and became a Christian himself.

Kyneburgha, like her brother Peada, became a Christian when she married into the royal family of Northumbria. After her husband's death, she returned to Mercia, where it is said that she and her sister Kyneswitha helped found the monastery at Medeshamstede. Her name is preserved in the name of the parish church at Castor which stands above the present-day village on the site of the Roman praetorium. She is said to have founded a religious establishment for men and women and although no trace of it remains, there is certainly evidence that wealthy Anglo-Saxons occupied the site.

Adulf became abbot after the rebuilding of the abbey in the tenth century. He had been chancellor to King Edgar but gave up his wealth and became a monk following the tragic death of his son. The child had been suffocated in his parents' bed as they slept off the effects of too much drink. Adulf told the king that rights had been granted to the first monastery. Edgar confirmed the Charters and paved the way for the Soke of Peterborough.

The legend of Saint Kyneburgha tells how she fled from three men who were intent on harming her. She prayed for deliverance and her prayers were answered when the men were swallowed up in a pit which opened behind her as she ran. Her own path was covered with flowers as she made her escape and she lived on to become known as a saintly woman, devoted to God. In the eleventh century the bones of Saints Kyneburgha, Kyneswitha and their relative Tibba were moved from Castor to the abbey in Burgh for safe keeping, in order to prevent the monks of Ramsey from taking them. It is possible that the religious house at Castor had been attacked by raiders as well, or at least fallen into disuse, as it is mentioned as being in ruins at that time.

OSWALD, KING AND MARTYR

Oswald was the Christian king of Northumbria in the seventh century and gave land to Bishop Aidan to found Lindisfarne. His holiness and generosity

The Hedda Stone – a Saxon sculpture from the first monastery.

were already well known in his lifetime and several stories were written about him during the eighth century by Bede in his (Ecclesiastical) *History of the English People*. He became king after setting up a wooden cross before leading his troops to victory at the Battle of Heaven's Field. Bede tells how Oswald and Aidan were eating an Easter meal when a message came to the king about a group of poor people asking for alms. Oswald gave them not only his food but also the silver dishes they were using. Aidan blessed the king, saying, 'May this arm never perish.'

When Oswald was killed in battle against Penda, king of Mercia, his dismembered body was taken by monks. It was said that the arm that had been blessed remained as it had been in life, and that miracles were performed in its presence. The arm was apparently stolen from Bamburgh by monks from Medeshamstede, where it became the most important relic in the monastery at the time, drawing many pilgrims to the shrine. St Oswald's Chapel can be seen in the cathedral today, built on the site of the high altar of the Saxon church.

In one corner of the chapel is a narrow watchtower where a monk could stand to watch over the precious relic night and day, in case anyone tried to steal it. It is in fact so narrow that the monk would be unable to sit, ensuring that he would keep awake at his post. Oswald's arm disappeared from the abbey at the time of the Reformation, along with other relics. It is possible that they were buried or taken by monks to protect them, though they may have been destroyed.

AD 1000

THE DANES AND THE NORMANS BATTLE FOR CONTROL

Death at the Gates of the Abbey

THE NAME OF Hereward is common around Peterborough to this day and has been used in the names of businesses, shops and even the local radio station. So who was the man who later became an English folk-hero, leader of those who fought the Normans in this area after the defeat of the Saxon king, Harold, at Hastings? In fact, very little is known for certain other than his alliance with the Danes against the Norman invaders, leading local rebels in a 'guerrilla' war from his base in the Fens. The addition of 'the Wake' to his name was made later and probably comes from a word meaning 'the watcher'. In his own lifetime he was known as Hereward the Outlaw or Hereward the Exile.

Most of the stories about Hereward the Wake appeared hundreds of years after his death, building on his reputation as a rebel leader fighting against the invaders. There are many theories as to who he was and what he achieved. Some accounts claim that his family owned land around Bourne in Lincolnshire and that Hereward was the nephew of the Saxon Abbot Brand of Peterborough, or indeed, the son of Earl Leofric and Lady Godiva, of Coventry fame. Some say he spent time in Europe after being banished, only returning to England after the defeat of King Harold.

In fact, the few details we know about Hereward are contained in an account written over two centuries after the events had taken place by Peterborough monk Hugh Candidus. The only mention of his origins comes in a brief but mysterious comment that he was 'a man of the monks'. Hugh wrote about a raid on the monastery and town by Danes and local Saxons who had been gathered together by Hereward to fight the Normans. The monks, hearing that their monastery was to be attacked, chose one of their community to go for help. He was to take as many of their valuables as he could carry and go to the Norman Abbot Turold, who was nearby in Stamford.

WILLIAM I

William the Conqueror: Hereward fought against his Norman armies.

Other treasures were hidden around the church and the gates and doors were closed as the monks prepared to defend themselves. The Danes and their local allies arrived by boat and tried to force their way into the abbey.

A fierce battle took place at the Bolhithe Gate as the monks fought to hold off their attackers. At first they were successful, but then the order was given to set fire to the gates and the surrounding buildings, opening the way for the rebels to enter the church. They made short work of plundering the treasures – items of gold, silver and precious stones were stolen, along with books and documents.

Meanwhile the fires had spread through all the monastery buildings and also through the small town at its gates. When Turold arrived with his Norman soldiers he found a scene of total devastation. No record was kept of how many were killed or injured, but it was noted that, apart from the monastery church itself, only one building remained standing. Turold was too late to pursue the Danes who had taken to their boats and headed for the Isle of Ely and safety. Hereward arrived there with the spoils of battle and several of the monks he had forced to go with him. The relics and treasures were divided between the Saxons and the Danes.

The most important relic stolen was St Oswald's arm, and as it had once been stolen from Bamburgh by a monk from Medeshamstede, so it was now stolen back by another. Waiting until the Danes were drunk and off their guard, he took the arm and hid it with some other relics and was able to smuggle them out to Ramsey Abbey for safe-keeping. The writer says that Hereward claimed to have taken the treasures only to save them from the Normans, intending to return them once the Saxons had driven them out.

Fearing that the Normans would hunt them down, the Danes took their plunder and sailed home, leaving Hereward to escape into the Fens with his followers.

Danes plundering the church.

FENLAND IN HEREWARD'S TIME

Peterborough sat on the edge of the Fens and the land, particularly to the east, consists of farmland, with rich, black, peaty soil excellent for producing crops. Since the draining of the Fens in the seventeenth century, the open views stretch for miles over large fields divided by the straight lines of drainage ditches and drove roads. In Hereward's day the landscape would have been quite different and it would have been easy for those trying to avoid capture to hide away.

Stretches of marshland and deeper water were interspersed with heavily wooded areas. Slightly higher patches of ground were joined together by causeways and paths, but it could be a dangerous area for those unfamiliar with the safe routes. The Normans would have found it almost impossible to follow Hereward and his rebels into the Fens without a local guide who knew the paths. It would have been easy to get lost or drown and certainly Norman soldiers would have proved quite easy targets for an ambush.

THE DEVIL TAKE IT!

The version of the *Anglo-Saxon Chronicle* which continued for the longest was that kept by Peterborough Abbey. The original manuscripts, written in the Anglo-Saxon language, were begun in the reign of King Alfred the Great of Wessex. Copies were then sent to monasteries around the country and the recording of events continued. As monasteries mainly wrote about what affected them, the contents differ; however, the manuscripts were sometimes lost, as in the great fire of 1116 at Burgh, and then updated from another version. The last part of the Peterborough version also shows how the English language had begun to change.

Abbot John de Séez supervised the rebuilding of the abbey church, our present-day cathedral. According to the chronicler, he had lost his temper with some monks in the refectory and cursed the monastery before leaving for his manor at Castor. Later, someone trying unsuccessfully to light a fire in the bakehouse shouted in frustration, 'The Devil take it!' – at which point the flames shot up. The fire supposedly burned for nine days, and destroyed houses in the town as well as most of the abbey buildings. John de Séez laid the foundation stone of the new abbey, our present-day cathedral, in 1118, and the beautiful pale limestone used in the construction was brought by barge from the quarries at Barnack.

PETERBOROUGH'S CASTLE

When Turold was abbot he asserted Norman authority over the monastery and town by building a motte and bailey castle on the north side of the monastery. The large mound which remains is visible in the Deanery Gardens today. It was known as Turold's Mount and would have been an earthwork with wooden structures.

HUGH CANDIDUS

Hugh Candidus wrote his history in the twelfth century, 500 years after the foundation of the first monastery. He himself witnessed events under four different abbots, including the fire of 1116. Another contributor to the Peterborough chronicle records the life and death of Hugh himself. When Hugh entered the monastery as a young boy he was frequently ill, bringing up bowls of blood. After one severe attack he was on the point of death. His brother monks were praying and weeping around him. Suddenly, he tried to speak. At last, he asked that a candle be lit for him on St Mary's altar, and vowed to pray there every day. Gradually his condition improved, and his recovery was seen as a miracle. He was a well-loved monk and he eventually became the sub-prior of the monastery. The name Candidus (white) referred to his fair hair and complexion.

AD 1100

THE ABBEY RISES AGAIN

'Built on the Blood of Becket'

AN EDICT WAS passed in the eighth century that every altar should contain a relic – something connected to a saint or a holy event.

From the earliest days of the Christian Church people had visited places and objects associated with saints. Tombs and relics such as a saint's bones or clothes drew pilgrims hoping to feel closer to God by entering the presence of holiness on earth.

It was believed that God would work through them to perform miracles. Small pieces of bone or hair, phials of blood or items associated with the saints or the life of Christ, were collected by Christian churches and monasteries. In addition, possession of a relic could reap huge financial rewards as pilgrims flocked to visit the place where they were kept and gave money to the Church. The demand for relics led to unscrupulous people claiming to have genuine items for sale. Today there are four places said

to possess the head of John the Baptist, for instance. Abbot Aelfsige was said to have been so keen to find relics to bring to Peterborough in the eleventh century that he 'worked like a laborious bee'!

Hugh Candidus, a monk of Peterborough in the twelfth century, lists some of the relics kept in the abbey at that time. The bones of local Saxon saints, Kyneburgha, Kineswitha and Tibba were venerated here, as was the arm of St Oswald. The long list includes small pieces of bone from the bodies of St Peter, St Paul and St Andrew, to whom the abbey church was dedicated, and dozens more saints. In addition, wrote Hugh, reliquaries held pieces of the cross upon which Christ was crucified, two pieces of His manger and cloth from the Virgin Mary's clothes, bread from the Feeding of the Five Thousand, a piece of St Wenceslas' hair shirt – and so on.

During the abbacy of Benedict in the late twelfth century, pilgrims came to Peterborough in such numbers and

Peterborough Bridge Fair in later years.

bringing such wealth that the building of the great nave was completed.

Abbot Benedict had been prior in Canterbury at the time Archbishop Thomas Becket was murdered. When he came to be abbot of Peterborough, money was needed to finish the magnificent Norman Church. Benedict brought with him a phial of Becket's blood and a piece of his rough shirt, stained with blood. He built a special chapel at the abbey gates to house the relics. Tiny drops of Becket's blood were said to have been added to water and sold to pilgrims. The building work continued and for this reason it was said that the nave had been 'built on Becket's blood'. Although the relics have long since disappeared, the beautiful Limoges casket in which they were kept and which depicts the martyrdom of Becket is now in the Victoria and Albert Museum in London. The chapel itself was partly demolished in the fifteenth century to provide stone for the new parish church of St John. The chancel of the chapel that remains in the precincts

on the left of the cathedral gates was once used as the King's School.

Benedict 'blessed in name and deed' was one of the first to suggest that Church silver should be given to help pay the ransom for King Richard I when he was held prisoner by the Duke of Austria and the Holy Roman Emperor. He had also raised the money to complete the rebuilding of the church.

THOMAS BECKET, SAINT AND MARTYR

Thomas Becket was born in 1118, the son of a wealthy merchant. He was well-educated and made rapid progress in his chosen career in the Church. Theobald, the Archbishop of Canterbury, recommended that he enter the king's service. Henry II was so impressed by Becket that he made him his chancellor and the two became great friends. Both had expensive tastes

The awful death of Thomas Becket.

23

and loved feasting, drinking, hunting and fighting in battle.

Henry had often disagreed with the power of the Church, and when Theobald died, he decided to make his friend archbishop in his place, despite opposition from the bishops and from Becket himself. Henry assumed that he would be able to remove some of the clergy's rights without any resistance. In fact, the opposite happened. From the moment he was appointed, Becket took his new responsibilities seriously. He gave away his wealth, turned his back on his former lifestyle and dedicated himself to the Church, living as the lowliest monk. Becket angered the king and his court by upholding Church laws and when the king threatened to put him on trial for treason, he had to flee to France.

The nave of Peterborough Cathedral – 'built on the blood of Becket'.

The disputes continued but eventually Becket returned to England, where he excommunicated those Church leaders who had supported Henry. The king, who was in Normandy at the time, was enraged by this challenge to his authority and allegedly shouted, 'Will no-one rid me of this turbulent priest?' Four men took him at his word and set sail for England, where they tried to get Thomas to change his mind. They found him celebrating Mass in Canterbury Cathedral, and when he refused to leave with them, they furiously attacked him and hacked him to death, smashing his skull with the force of their blows. The site of his death and his tomb immediately became a place of pilgrimage and the Pope made him a saint.

Henry himself had to seek the Church's forgiveness and Becket's murderers were ordered to go to the Holy Land for fourteen years. The cult of Thomas Becket, martyr, spread throughout Europe and it is not surprising that the relics in Peterborough's abbey drew so many pilgrims to the town.

It would be surprising if the local population did not benefit from their presence and their custom as the abbey benefited from its association with Becket.

AD 1300

THE PEASANTS' REVOLT!

The Fighting Bishop Rides to the Rescue!

THE BLACK DEATH swept through England in the early part of the fourteenth century, wiping out so many people that whole villages were left deserted. Those who owed service to their feudal lord in return for their livelihood died in such numbers that lords of the manor could not get enough people to work the land. Crops could not be gathered and animals were left to wander through the countryside, often dying because there was no one left to tend them.

Landowners were so desperate for people to work in the fields that they often agreed to free their serfs and meet their demands for more money and the right to work where they liked. It was the first time that peasants felt they had enough power to get what they wanted. The inhabitants of Peterborough worked for their lord the abbot, and the majority of them were agricultural labourers. Many people in town would be working in the wool industry, combing, cleaning

and spinning the wool coming from the thousands of sheep kept on the common lands around the town.

In other parts of England, people were using the crisis to fight for more rights and a freer life. A new law restricted the amount of money a peasant could earn – and, at the same time, a new tax was levied to help pay for a war against France. The Poll Tax meant that everyone over the age of fifteen had to pay an extra shilling, more than farm labourers could afford. Matters came to a head in 1381 when tax collectors were assaulted by villagers refusing to pay the Poll Tax. Led by Wat Tyler, protestors reached London, where the rebellion was finally crushed.

In Peterborough in the same year, the abbey came under attack from tenants demanding their rights. The monks were in great danger of being overwhelmed and it seemed that the townspeople would manage to break into the abbey until the arrival of Henry le Despencer,

Misericord of Henry Despencer, the Fighting Bishop.

Bishop of Norwich. Known as the 'Fighting Bishop', it was rumoured that he always wore armour under his robes so as to be ready for battle. He had trained as a soldier and fought in several campaigns. He had a reputation for ruthlessness and had no hesitation in executing those who opposed him. He was returning to Norwich from Stamford when he heard about the storming of the abbey.

Although he initially had only sixteen soldiers with him, he rode to the rescue, gathering more fighting men on the way.

He rode straight into the mob gathered at the abbey gates and killed several men, hacking them down with his sword and driving them away. Some tried to take refuge in the chapel of St Thomas Becket but they too were slaughtered. Once he had subdued the revolt, he stayed long enough to hang the ringleaders before he returned to Norwich.

A MARVELLOUS FURY OF ANGER!

One of many disputes between those in the town and those in the abbey led to a near riot when a noisy mob of about forty people 'in great marvellous fury of anger' gathered at the gates of the monastery. A monk called Dan William Boston came upon the angry crowd when he was making his way to the 'checker' to pay in money. Trying to calm them down, the monk offered the protestors a drink, which they refused. A quarrel broke out between the abbot's servant, Thomas Wheatley, and Walter Baker, church warden of the parish church. Baker threatened to attack Wheatley if he came out of the abbey gates – which, of course, he didn't.

Dan William, now addressing the rioters through a window from the safety of the checker building, tried to calm the situation again. He admonished two men, Robert and Peter Edward, who were abusing the abbot and calling him 'the devil'. The monk accused them of speaking in an 'unmannerly way', unworthy of how honest men should speak of the absent 'honest prelate', the abbot. Peter Edwards, obviously ready for a fight, told the monk to come out and shut him up if he didn't like what he was saying. Reminding Edwards that he was 'a religious man and a priest', he declined the offer!

LIFE IN THE TOWN

Markets and fairs played a large part in the life of Peterborough in the Middle Ages. The right to hold a market and to charge a toll on all goods going through the town was a source of great wealth. Markets were held at the abbey gates and many traders and pedlars would travel to sell their wares in the town. The Pie Powder Court or the Court of Pieds Poudreux (dusty feet) dealt with disputes and troublemakers on market or fair days. The 'dusty feet' could have referred to travellers who had come to town on business or pleasure or possibly to those who walked round the market to monitor behaviour.

The clerk of the market judged cases brought before him, though as there were no set fines he could line his own pocket if he so chose. The cases were heard either in the market itself or possibly in the old Moot House or in a room above the abbey gates. Both these buildings were right next to the market place and those involved could be swiftly brought to justice and punishment carried out immediately. The guilty party would probably have to pay a fine or have property confiscated if they could not come up with the money. An alternative punishment might mean spending time in the stocks which were set up in the market place. The majority of those who appeared before the court would be involved in disputes about the quality and weight of goods on sale, including whether animals were fit to be sold. Theft and fights were similarly dealt with on the day of the market as many of those accused would not actually live in the town.

From the twelfth century Peterborough had been entitled to hold fairs. St Peter's Fair (Cherry Fair), St Oswald's Fair, and Bridge Fair drew people from all over the country. The fairs were held on Fair Meadows by the River Nene and had their own rules and regulations. It was possible to get married at the fair, or settle disputes. It was said that travelling people would settle arguments between themselves at the Peterborough Fair because it was so big no one would intervene. Drunkenness and fights were common, but only one murder was known to have been committed – a body was found in bushes by the river, but no one was ever caught. It would have been hard to know what went on, as most of the people there would just be passing through.

The drudgery and harshness of every day life meant that any form of entertainment – however cruel and unpleasant it may seem to us – was welcomed. The barbaric practice of bull baiting was actually a legal requirement in Peterborough. A butcher who slaughtered an animal which had not

Cock fighting, a popular sport in the area at this time.

been baited by dogs would be subject to a fine. The original reason for baiting an animal before it was butchered was to make the meat tender. A bull would be tethered to an iron ring attached to a chain which was long enough to allow some movement. Dogs would be released to taunt and attack the bull, which would often turn on the dogs and injure or kill them. Gradually, this practice developed into a 'sport' where bets were placed on which dog would do the most damage. Bull-running was always looked on as sport and usually happened on special occasions to celebrate an important event. A young bull or a heifer was released in Market Square then chased by people and dogs until it was too exhausted to run any more. The chase usually ended in the meadows by the river where the unfortunate animal would be killed. The last recorded instance of this form of animal cruelty in Peterborough was in 1799.

Cock fighting was a popular sport right up to the end of the eighteenth century. Sharp spurs were tied to the cockerels' legs and they were placed in an enclosed area or pit to fight to the death. Both birds would be slashed by the spurs but eventually one would have so many wounds that it would bleed to death. The Angel Inn had a cock pit, and although the sport was banned in 1792 it is believed to have continued for some time after that.

Drinking, gambling and fighting provided entertainment when nothing else was happening. Public punishments always drew huge crowds who enjoyed taunting those sentenced to the stocks or a whipping. The Abbey Courts' book records many incidents that took place in the streets which no doubt caused great amusement to onlookers.

At regular intervals, all men between the ages of fifteen and sixty were required by law to attend archery practise at the town practise butts. The first of these laws was passed in 1252 and meant that they were prepared to fight when called upon.

DISEASE

The streets were filthy, smelly and breeding grounds for disease. Beggars and orphaned children lived and died amongst the rubbish and those disfigured by disease would often be driven away. Leprosy was one of the illnesses which caused most revulsion.

Lepers were condemned to live away from the rest of society, wearing clothes that distinguished them from other people and carrying a bell to warn of their presence. Like many other illnesses in the Middle Ages, leprosy was often seen as being a punishment for sin. It was the Church authorities who set up Leper Hospitals on the edges of towns where infection could be contained. Although symptoms could take years to develop, in those days it was an incurable disease and the hideous physical effects of leprosy caused disgust and terror. At the time, other types of skin disease were often confused with leprosy. Being sent to the Lazar or Leprosy Hospital meant certain death. Spital Bridge in Peterborough takes its name from the days when St Leonard's Hospital for Lepers was built here. Overcrowded, squalid houses without any access to fresh water and sanitation meant disease spread quickly. Many children died in infancy and women often died in childbirth. Any open wound would quickly get infected because of such dirty conditions and lack of understanding about how illnesses came about. Life was often short and brutal, and sufferings of fellow human beings or animals often did not affect people whose own situation hardened them against most forms of cruelty.

AD 1400

LIFE IN THE ABBEY

Saints or Sinners?

PEOPLE BECAME MONKS for a variety of reasons in the Middle Ages. Entering a Benedictine foundation like Peterborough Abbey meant that you left behind the outside world and your possessions in it. You could not leave the abbey without your abbot's permission and your days would be taken up with prayer, the worship of God, study and work. Most chose the life of a monk in order to devote their lives to God but there would have been others who found the monastery a haven from the troubles and harshness of life outside their enclosed world. However lowly your situation in life, you might rise to a position of power; certainly an abbot was a powerful figure in the Middle Ages.

From time to time the Bishop of Lincoln would visit the abbey and report on life there. The monks would be reminded that they should not allow women into the monastery, nor pawn jewels, and must maintain silence as far as possible. These instructions imply

A Benedictine monk. (With the kind permission of the Thomas Fisher Rare Book Library, University of Toronto)

that they were not all behaving properly. In 1360 monks were granted a pardon after attacking some lay members of the monastery. One can only imagine what led to them being accused in the first place! They had to be reprimanded again after 'encouraging' people to visit the tomb of a convicted criminal, Lawrence of Oxford. They claimed that miracles had been performed at the tomb and suggested that gifts of money would be very welcome.

During the time of Abbot Kirkton, from 1496 to 1528, the monks complained to the visiting Bishop of Lincoln about the way he ran the abbey. He had moved the service of Matins to a much earlier time, making them get up during the night. He supposedly neglected the education of the novices and had allowed part of the abbey, including the dorter (dormitory), vaults and farmery (belonging to the abbey farm) to deteriorate to a 'ruinous' state. His deer park had blocked the monks' direct route to the farm and lands

at Oxney, where it appears they liked to go for relaxation from abbey life, as well as work. In the thirteenth century a history of the abbey noted that monks went to Oxney for 'blood letting' and relaxation, presumably if they had been ill.

The food at that time was also supposed to have been better, as you might expect from being fresh from the land. By Kirkton's time, monks were complaining about poor food, bad meat, fish that wasn't fresh and watery ale. (Beer was, of course, the usual drink, being much safer than water, and the monks had an allowance every day.)

At Oxney things seem to have been worse for those who were sick as they complained that they received only a pennyworth of food a day. Neither could an invalid expect much comfort as there were no single beds for them. Those who were not ill were no better off as there was no separate area for patients with infectious diseases, thus making the spread of infection inevitable.

It is chiefly for the New Building at the east end of the cathedral that we remember Kirkton today. He oversaw the construction of the so-called New Building which extended the church beyond the original Apse and included the beautiful fan-vaulted ceiling. Its style is in marked contrast to the Norman church and certainly imprinted Kirkton's name on the history of the building.

Kirkton's rebus (a picture in stone, representing words) of a robin (Robert) and a kirk (or church) on a tun (barrel) – i.e. Kirkton – appears around the New Building, emphasizing who was responsible for the work. The Tudor Rose was used in his building projects to compliment the monarchy. In 1503 he was summoned to appear before the king charged with hunting on the king's land without permission. Fortunately for Kirkton, he had a powerful friend, Lady Margaret Beaufort, grandmother of Henry VIII. Her favourite house (and for some time the home of Henry Fitzroy, the monarch's illegitimate son) was close by at Collyweston.

The Kirkton gate in the cathedral precincts, formerly the entrance to the deer park.

Instead of appointing others to the various posts within the monastery, Kirkton kept many for himself, drawing the income they brought without doing the necessary work. The monks, on the other hand, did not seem to mind the fact that the sub-cellarer provided a sort of 'bar' where they could have wine till seven in winter and eight in summer. They were reprimanded for taking food to give as presents to people in the town, not even to the poor and needy, but presumably to friends or as payment for services rendered. They had to be told to go to bed earlier as they were often not awake enough to fully participate in services.

It was also reported that the older monks did not set a good example, misbehaving in the choir, whilst the Sacristan neglected the estates and woodland for which he was responsible. He had also stolen jewels from St Oswald's Shrine to give to female friends. Other monks were told to refrain from returning to the dormitory, singing drunkenly, and disturbing those who were already asleep. Perhaps it is no wonder that the abbot required attendance at earlier services!

Visiting entertainers seem to have performed at the abbey, as from 1444 to 1446 money was paid to 'strolling players'. It is possible that they had been there for the enjoyment of some of the abbey's important guests.

The arrival of an important guest at the abbey brought trade for the townspeople, and the excitement of seeing the finery of the entourage; although great personages travelled with most of their own goods (including furniture!), there would still be extra work and income for the townspeople.

Not long before the Dissolution of the Monasteries, Cardinal Wolsey stayed in Peterborough Abbey to celebrate Easter. Wolsey had been lord chancellor and chief advisor to Henry VIII but had fallen from favour because of his failure to secure Henry's divorce from Katharine of Aragon. He had been allowed to remain Archbishop of York and was travelling there in 1530 when he stayed at Peterborough Abbey. It was recorded that he arrived with 160 followers and twelve carts carrying what he needed for his journey. Apart from the extra food, drink and goods that would be bought locally, fifty-nine poor people were given generous gifts on Maundy Thursday.

They each received twelve pence, though the lucky fifty-ninth had twenty-four pence. Each had three ells (nearly three and a half metres) of canvas to make a shirt, a new pair of shoes and a cask of red herrings.

Following the week of services at the abbey, Wolsey requested permission to visit his old friend Sir William Fitzwilliam while he was in Peterborough. The tradesmen were paid for their services and told that any complaint against the cardinal's servants would be dealt with. He was welcomed to Milton Hall and told that he need not unpack any of his furniture 'unless it were my lorde's bedd, for his own person'. Henry had ordered that the disgraced cardinal must not be received in any individual's house, so a large tent was erected in the grounds and furnished for his comfort.

Entertaining guests caused great expense and the monks appealed for extra income from the ownership of more lands. Warmington church was given over to the abbey to increase funds. One particular visit of the future Edward II recorded as costing £1,543 13s 4d. This included not only the cost of feeding Edward and his retinue but also the expensive presents which were expected to be presented to the royal visitor. The abbot gave Edward a richly decorated cloak but he refused to accept it until his favourite, Piers Gaveston, had been given one too.

AD 1500

THE REFORMATION

The Sad End of a Loyal Queen

ON 29 JANUARY 1537 the funeral service of Katharine of Aragon was held in the great abbey of St Peter in the city of Peterborough. The ceremony did not celebrate Katharine as queen of England but only as the widow of Prince Arthur, elder brother of Henry VIII, who had died before becoming king of England. Katharine's subsequent marriage to Henry had been deemed unlawful and their daughter Mary declared illegitimate. Mary was not allowed to attend her mother's funeral and Eustace Chapuys, the imperial ambassador who had long championed Katharine's cause, refused to attend because she was not to be buried as queen. The sad and lonely end to her tragic life was in stark contrast to her arrival in England at the age of fifteen.

Katharine was the daughter of King Ferdinand and Queen Isabella of Spain, destined to be the bride of Arthur, the heir to the English throne. She was well-received by the English who looked to profitable trading links with Spain. She had not been married long when Arthur died; her marriage to his younger brother Henry was eventually celebrated after special dispensation from the Pope. She loved dancing and hunting but was well-educated and hard-working, and her charitable works made her very popular with the English people.

When Henry was away in France, Katharine helped run the country and also served for some years as Spanish ambassador in England. However, this was not enough to ensure a successful marriage. Two children died at or soon after birth, and rumours of Henry's affairs began; a third child was to die at birth before Katharine had a healthy daughter, Mary. Her continuing failure to produce a son, ill-health and Henry's loss of interest in her meant that she became more and more isolated, especially when Mary was sent away from court. By now Henry was

Henry VIII and his wives. Katharine is at the top, directly above Henry, with the cross about her neck.

Even the thought of her death would not make Katharine deny her marriage and eventually the king's men withdrew.

The former queen was now moved to Kimbolton Castle, a fortified manor house closer to Peterborough. Her staff was reduced again and she refused to deal with those who did not call her queen. She locked herself away in her rooms with her few loyal companions, only eating what was prepared for her there. Her great concern was for the safety of her daughter and, desperate to see her, she requested a meeting with her. However, her rapidly declining health did not soften Henry's heart and she was never to see her daughter again, or leave Kimbolton alive. On her deathbed she wrote to Henry, still declaring her love:

My most dear lord, king and husband: The hour of my death now drawing on, the tender love I owe you forceth me, my case being such, to commend myself to you, and to put you in remembrance with a few words of the health and safeguard of your soul which you ought to prefer before all worldly matters, and before the care and pampering of your body, for the which you have cast me into many calamities and yourself into many troubles. For my part, I pardon you everything, and I wish to devoutly pray God that He will pardon you also. For the rest, I commend unto you our daughter Mary, beseeching you to be a good father unto her, as I have heretofore desired. I desire you also, on behalf of my maids, to give them marriage portions, which is not much, they being but three. For all my other

looking for a way to divorce Katharine in order to marry Anne Boleyn. He was helped in this by Cardinal Wolsey, the lord chancellor, who had always seen Katharine as a threat to his own power. Declaring himself head of the Church in England, Henry stated that his marriage to Katharine was invalid because she had previously been his brother's wife.

Katharine's small household was moved to Ampthill, and then to Buckden in Huntingdonshire, which was damp and unpleasant in winter. The king's representatives came to inform her that she and her household must swear an oath that her first marriage was illegal, under threat of treason if they refused.

Katharine's monument in the cathedral.

servants I solicit the wages due them, and a year more, lest they be unprovided for. Lastly, I make this vow, that mine eyes desire you above all things.

In 1541 the abbey church became a cathedral, one of only six such churches to survive the destruction of the monasteries. Undoubtedly the move from abbey to cathedral church was made easier by the last abbot, John Chambers, but it has been suggested that part of the reason was because Katharine had been buried there. It appears that Chambers was quick to offer the abbey to the king after the Reformation, and he was appointed the first bishop of the new diocese.

A visitor to the site in 1640 declared that he had been miraculously cured of a growth on his forehead thanks to the intercession of Katharine. He had dreamt of a black hearse and a marble slab where there were drops of water with which he was to wet his forehead. On seeing the tomb of the queen, he dipped his finger into a drop of water there; a week later, he claimed to have been cured.

During the Civil War, the original monument above the burial place was destroyed and not fully replaced until the turn of the nineteenth century. Katherine Clayton was the wife of a cathedral canon who helped organise a nationwide collection from other Katherines in order to provide a new monument in honour of the Tudor queen. The standards of Aragon, Castile and Leon and the royal standard of Henry VIII were hung above the memorial at the request of Queen Mary of Teck, wife of King George V. Above her tomb in Peterborough are the words 'Katharine, Queen of England', so that in death her true title was restored to her. Her memory is still honoured by an annual service celebrating her life and by the placing of flowers and pomegranates (her personal emblem) on her tomb. In life, 'humble and loyal', in death, remembered as a faithful queen.

AD 1587

ROYAL RIVALS

The Awful Execution of Mary, Queen of Scots

PRIOR TO HER burial in Peterborough Cathedral on the first of August 1587, the embalmed body of Mary, Queen of Scots, had lain in a lead coffin at her place of execution in Fotheringhay Castle. Immediately after her beheading, her body had been carried to another room and hastily covered by a piece of cloth torn from a billiard table. Such was the undignified end of the woman who became queen of Scotland at only one week old and then, after marrying the heir to the French throne, queen of France at the age of sixteen.

Her life at the French court ended after the death of Francis II, her husband, and she returned to Scotland. As in England at the time, there was some opposition to a Roman Catholic monarch. She later married Lord Darnley and gave birth to a son, James. Darnley's desire for power and his jealousy of Mary's Italian secretary, Rizzio, drove him to arrange

Mary, Queen of Scots was the granddaughter of Henry VII's daughter Margaret. Many Roman Catholics in England and Scotland believed that she had more right to be queen of England than Elizabeth, daughter of Henry VIII and his second wife, Anne Boleyn. Mary's Roman Catholic supporters thought that Henry's divorce and remarriage had been illegal.

In their eyes, Elizabeth was illegitimate and not entitled to the English throne. During the nineteen years Mary was in England Elizabeth had resisted attempts to have her executed, although she was the focus of many plots to restore her to the Scottish throne and crown her queen of England. It was Mary's implication in a plot involving her friend Sir Anthony Babington that sealed her fate and drove Elizabeth to sign her death warrant.

The execution of Mary, Queen of Scots.

prisoner for many years. After some evidence of plots against her, Elizabeth finally signed Mary's death warrant.

On the night before her execution Mary wrote that she had been denied her priest and that her religion was the real reason she was to be killed. As she prepared to enter the hall where the sentence was to be carried out, her companions were told they could not stay with her. Eventually, it was agreed that she could choose six people to enter the hall with her. Mary appeared quite calm as she approached the block and continued her prayers despite an attempt by the dean of Peterborough Cathedral to get her to renounce her Catholic faith at the last. About 300 people crowded into the hall as witnesses to her gruesome death.

According to one of those present, the executioner appeared to have an ordinary axe such as those used for chopping wood. Certainly the blade did not do its job immediately. The first blow missed her neck and hit her head. Those present heard the queen say 'Sweet Jesus' before the axe struck again. Even the second blow did not sever her head completely and the executioner raised the axe for a third time. As the head fell to the floor, he took hold of the long hair to raise it to the crowd and instead lifted the auburn wig she had been wearing to hide her own short grey hair. The dean of Peterborough shouted, 'So perish all the enemies of Queen Elizabeth'. Her little dog was found hiding under her skirts and her own ladies were not allowed near her body as it was prepared for burial.

for his brutal murder in front of the queen. His own death by strangulation the following year, after an explosion at the house where he was staying, was seen by many as the work of Mary and Boswell, the man who became her third husband. Public opinion forced her to abdicate in favour of her son and she fled to England, hoping to enlist the help of her cousin Elizabeth I. Elizabeth feared the Roman Catholic queen and her claim to the English throne and Mary was kept

Twenty-five years after her burial in Peterborough Cathedral her son James, now king of Scotland and England, ordered that her body should be reinterred in Westminster Abbey and that Fotheringhay be razed to the ground. Among the furnishings removed from the castle was the staircase down which Mary walked to her execution. It was removed to the Talbot Inn in Oundle where her ghost is said to walk to this day.

FOTHERINGHAY

Fotheringhay Castle was the birthplace of Richard III and had a long association with the royal House of York. When Katharine of Aragon wanted to leave the damp and uncomfortable manor house of Buckden, Henry considered sending her to Fotheringhay, which she had always hated. She was eventually taken to Kimbolton Castle, to the south of Peterborough.

ROYAL GRAVES AND A ROYAL GRAVEDIGGER

On either side of the huge west door of Peterborough Cathedral are pictures of gravedigger Robert Scarlett who lived in the sixteenth century. The painting on the left as you enter was copied from the original wall painting on the right and hangs above the grave marker of

Kimbolton Castle, which was home to Katharine of Aragon until her death.

Old Scarlett, the Peterborough sexton.

the man who claimed to have buried two generations of townspeople. Robert Scarlett was sexton of St John's, Peterborough's parish church, and of the abbey of St Peter, later the cathedral. As he lived to the age of ninety-eight and was known for his strength it is not unlikely that his claim was true – especially as there had been an outbreak of plague in the town.

He lived in the market place at the abbey gates. His first wife Margaret died in 1584 but he remarried at the age of eighty-nine, wedding a woman named Maud Gosling. He is best remembered, however, for another reason. In 1537 he buried Queen Katharine of Aragon, and in 1587 was still active enough to bury, or at least supervise the burial of, Mary, Queen of Scots.

The dean of the cathedral at this time was Dean Fletcher, who had been present at Fotheringhay Castle to witness the execution of the Scottish queen. Dean Fletcher's son, John, was a well-known playwright and friend of William Shakespeare. They worked together on Shakespeare's *The Famous History of the Life of King Henry the Eighth*, among other plays. As Scarlett was such a well-known local figure at the time and obviously quite a remarkable character, it has been suggested that he may have provided some of the inspiration for the gravedigger in Shakespeare's *Hamlet*.

The following lines about him were probably written by John Fletcher:

You see old Scarlitt's picture stand on hie,

But at your feete here doth his body lye.

His gravestone doth his age and Death time show,

His office by thes tokens you may know.

Second to none for strength and sturdye limm,

A Scarebabe mighty voice with visage grim.

Hee had interd two Queenes within this place

And this townes Householders in his lives space

Twice over: But at length his own time came;

What for others did for him the same

Was done: No doubt his soule doth live for aye

In heaven: Tho here his body clad in clay.

AD 1600

THE CIVIL WAR YEARS

Destruction and a Horrific Death

ALTHOUGH NO MAJOR battles were fought in the immediate area, there are reminders of that violent period of England's history in the city. Royalist strongholds in the north and the Fens, including a garrison at Crowland, made Peterborough a good place to station troops. Seeing the great cathedral as a symbol of 'popery' and of the power and riches of the established Church and monarchy, parliamentary soldiers were determined to destroy as much of it as they could. The consequences of their actions can still be seen today.

Whilst their commanding officer took over The Vineyard, a large house in the cathedral precincts, his soldiers stabled their horses inside the church. They used the beautifully painted ceiling of the Apse for target practice, firing their muskets repeatedly to obliterate the pictures of the saints. Paintings, stained glass and monuments were regarded as idolatry and symbols of popery. The stone spires of the High Altar were pulled down with ropes and the rubble left where it fell. So thorough was their destruction of the famous windows of the cloisters that only small pieces of glass remained. The cloister windows had been recorded as depicting scenes from the Old and New Testaments, the history of the abbey and of English kings. Some of the shattered fragments were gathered together and placed in the windows above the Apse – faces of Jesus, the apostles and other saints, angels' wings, leaves and birds show what was lost. Amongst the monuments that were smashed was the tomb of Katharine of Aragon.

Another notable monument of which very little remains belonged to Sir Humphrey Orme, one of Peterborough's MPs and a Royalist. Sir Humphrey had commissioned the memorial to be built in his lifetime and lived to witness parliamentarians smash it with hammers then parade an effigy of him through the town.

Documents and books were torn up as they were thought to have come from the Pope. Fortunately one of the early histories of the abbey, dating back to the thirteenth century, was bought from a soldier by one of the cathedral's 'singing men', Humphrey Austin, for ten shillings. The receipt, written out by the soldier, who had been told that the book was a Latin Bible, is still in the book today.

Stones from what was left of the Lady Chapel were sold or used to repair some of the damage elsewhere. Oliver St John, Lord Chief Justice and a relative of Cromwell, took some stone to build Thorpe Hall, which is about a mile from the city centre. Thorpe Hall was one of the few great houses to be built during the Commonwealth and today is a Sue Ryder Home. A reminder of the source of some of the building materials came to light when workmen found carvings on the back of stones set into the wall, hiding their original use.

The cathedral, attacked by Roundheads during the Civil War. (LC-DIG-ppmsc-08781)

... DANGER

It was some time before the cathedral could be used again for worship. Heaps of rubble lay on the floor where the altars and monuments had been smashed into pieces. Two young boys had a lucky escape whilst playing in the abandoned church. They decided to go through the hole where the bell ropes hung and swing down to the ground. Both fell, but amazingly they survived. Another boy, hunting for jackdaws' nests, was not so lucky – the rotten boards of the roof gave way and he crashed to his death.

... AND DEATH

One of the more horrific events of the Civil War took place at a fortified manor house to the west of the town on 6 June 1648. A local Royalist supporter, Dr Michael Hudson, had led a group of men against the Parliamentarians but had been forced to flee. They took refuge in Woodcroft Castle, where they were unable to hold off their pursuers. A contemporary account by a certain Anthony Wood reveals what happened next:

After the rebels (Parliamentarians) had entered the house and had taken most of the Royalists, Hudson, with some of his courageous soldiers, went up to the battlements thereof, where they defended themselves for some time. At length, upon promise of quarter, they yielded; but when the rebels got in among them, they denied to make it good. Whereupon Hudson, being thrown over the battlements, caught hold of a spout or overstone and there hung. But his hands being beat or cut off, he fell into the moat underneath, much wounded and desired to come onto land to die there. Whereupon one Egbourne... knocked him on the head with the butt of his musket. Which being done, one Walker, a chandler or grocer in Stamford, cut out his tongue and carried it about the county, as a trophy.

Civil war musketeer. A gun like this was used to smash the skull of Dr Michael Hudson.

It is said that on the night of 6 June every year, the sounds of battle and the screams of Hudson pleading for mercy can be heard still. His is not the only apparition said to haunt the site. A lady, believed to be his fiancée and witness to his terrible death, walks the grounds on 25 July – the day they had planned to marry.

THE CORPSE OF CROMWELL

Oliver Cromwell was born in Huntingdon and was elected MP there. He was a very successful cavalry commander and later became commander in chief of the parliamentary army fighting against the king's forces during the Civil War. He was a man of deep faith in God and a staunch Protestant. He refused the crown after the execution of Charles I and became Lord Protector of England until his death in 1658 and burial in Westminster Abbey.

Charles II was invited back to become king two years later and Cromwell's body was dug up so that he could be 'executed' at Tyburn for High Treason. The headless corpse was thrown into a common burial pit whilst his head was put on a stake. Sidney Sussex College in Cambridge, where Cromwell had been a student, claim that his head was later buried in the college grounds.

Cromwell's widow, Elizabeth, lived with members of her family at Northborough Hall outside Peterborough and is buried in the churchyard there.

AD 1665

THE PLAGUE STRIKES AGAIN!

Pestilence Devastates the Local Population

ALTHOUGH THE WORST outbreak of plague in Peterborough occurred in 1665, there had been frequent outbreaks of this terrifying disease, from the thirteenth century 'Black Death' to the seventeenth century 'Great Plague'. In the fourteenth century over half the monks in Peterborough Abbey died, as well as many in the town and the surrounding countryside.

The outbreak seems to have entered Britain through the busy ports of western England before raging through the country, virtually wiping out some communities. Whole households died within a few days of one another, the survivors forced to watch as their loved ones succumbed to the horrible symptoms. Painful swellings which turned from red to black appeared on various parts of the body; high temperatures, sickness and internal bleeding followed. Victims died within two to four days of falling ill and whole households

were wiped out within a few days of one another. Although rat fleas passed on one type of plague to humans, the disease could also be passed from person to person by the coughs which characterised another form of plague. The number of deaths in such a short space of time meant that church burial grounds could not cope, and people were buried on their own property. Fear of plague also meant that people were buried away from the town in plague pits, where bodies would be hurriedly thrown in.

The vicar of the Peterborough parish church of St John the Baptist, Simon Gunton, was the only clergyman to remain in post during the plague years of 1665 to 1667, whilst other clergy made excuses to leave. He is also remembered for recording details of Peterborough Cathedral before it was damaged in the Civil War. He noted the names of those who died, marking each with a cross to denote the cause of death and at the foot of some pages including

Contemporary views from Hollar's 'Dance of Death', showing death coming for the monk and for the commoner alike. (With kind permission of the Thomas Fisher Rare Book Library, University of Toronto)

a prayer of thanks in Latin for his own preservation, such as *Gratia & bonitate Dei salvus*, 'saved by the goodness and grace of God'. The short phrases of thanks to God convey both his great faith and his relief at being spared when so many of his congregation had been struck down. As on previous occasions it appears that the plague was brought by a visitor from London but it spread so quickly that churches could not keep up with the burials. Churchyards and cemeteries did not have room for more victims so permission was given for other places to be used. Entries in the parish register show such places as 'in their yard', 'in a garden', 'in their orchard' or 'in the fenwash'.

Gunton lost over 400 of his parishioners, a third of the population at that time. Most victims would have been buried at the Pesthouse but the exact location of this building is not known, though clues from the feoffees' records imply that it was somewhere in the Westgate area of town. One rental agreement concerned a residence and land in Westgate 'near the Pesthouse'.

In 1668 it was noted that wood from the buildings used during the latest outbreak was to be taken down and stored in the belfry of St John's church. It would seem likely that the wooden buildings had been used and dismantled before and that they were expected to be needed again in the future.

Evidence of mass burials further away from the centre of town was unearthed in the 1950s, when builders working on land about a mile from the city centre uncovered hundreds of bones. There were stone coffins in one area but the number of skeletons piled on top of one another led to the conclusion that this was a plague pit. There was no record of a cemetery around St John's in the centre of town but several skeletons were found during landscaping work in 2011.

The original parish church had been located behind the cathedral in the old Saxon settlement and had continued in use even when the 'New Town' of the early twelfth century was built. It was not until the fifteenth century that stones from that church and from the Becket Chapel at the cathedral gates had been used to build a new parish church, right in the middle of the market place. It had always been assumed that no graveyard had been sited round the new church. There had certainly been some sort of garden there at a later date but any cemetery there could not have been used for long. The remains were dated to the fifteenth century and have now been reburied.

Once plague had entered a household the door was marked with a large red cross and the inhabitants locked inside to prevent them spreading the infection. Although this practice seemingly condemned everyone within the house to death, it was not always the case that every member of the household succumbed to the infection. On 24 October 1630, at the request of Sir Humphrey Orme, the feoffees made a charitable payment of five shillings for the relief of Laurence Pierson. His house had been sealed off and marked with the dreaded red cross since 'he had entertained a stranger that dyed, and suspected to be of the plague'.

In 1606 a visitor from London fell ill and died in the home of one William Browne. William, two of his children and a servant died, but his wife and her maid, although falling victim to the disease, escaped with 'sores'. St John's parish registers show family members dying within a few days of each other and we can only imagine the horror of those who had not yet succumbed watching loved ones die, knowing that the same fate probably awaited them too. James Cofield, his daughter Rose and wife Elizabeth were all buried on the same day, 2 August 1666. Another daughter, Mary, was buried on the thirteenth of the same month. John Brimrose and his sister Elizabeth were also buried on 2 August, their father and mother soon afterwards.

AD 1560-1800

THE FEOFFEES

Workhouses and the Wretched Poor

IN **1561, A** body of men known as the feoffees took over responsibility for the care of the poor and needy in the town. Whereas before the Dissolution of the Monasteries the abbot had acted as Lord of the Manor, that role passed to the dean and chapter of the new cathedral. When Elizabeth I came to the throne, a Poor Law compelled parishes to look after the elderly, infirm and orphans using money from a tax on businessmen or property owners in the town. Church lands had been confiscated, but when the land came onto the market, three Peterborough men of business bought it back on behalf of the town.

A charitable trust was set up to use the income from the property for helping the poor as well as for maintaining the parish church, roads and town bridge. The feoffees were those who were appointed to run the charitable trust and their number varied from four to fourteen. At times they were slow to bring their numbers up to fourteen again and

they were criticised for not doing their job properly. Although they received donations, it was difficult to carry out all their duties; at one time they issued

There were many beggar women in Peterborough, including the 'miserable creatures' described overleaf. (With kind permission of the Thomas Fisher Rare Book Library, University of Toronto)

The Guild Hall, meeting place of the feoffees.

'a miserable creature', was given money on several occasions, notably 'towards paying her Chyurgien', as she had been 'long infested with the pox'.

In 1630, two shillings and sixpence hopefully relieved the suffering of Gilbert Clarke, a thatcher who had fallen from a roof while working and 'was thereby maimed'. Clothes and shoes were provided for boys starting out as apprentices, money for buying bread went to adults and children and, highlighting the wretched conditions of abandoned or orphaned children, several entries record the provision of a 'winding sheet' or shroud for the burial of a child found dead on the streets.

Their other financial responsibilities meant that the feoffees made payments for work done such as digging gravel, mending buckets belonging to the Church, for mending shoes and moving the dunghills from the narrow streets.

The mention of the thatcher reminds us that the majority of buildings in the town were constructed of wood and thatched. Only the houses of the wealthier inhabitants would have any stone used in their construction. There was no source of stone available in the immediate area of the town. Only those who could afford it could pay to have stone brought by barge from quarries some miles away. For this reason, fires were a great hazard and few examples of early housing are left in Peterborough.

Human and household waste was thrown out into the streets and stallholders in the Marketstede were often fined for leaving rubbish or

Peterborough Halfpenny tokens enabling them to put off cash payments till they drew the annual income from rents.

The majority of the charitable payments distributed by the feoffees were given to the old and infirm or to widows and orphans who had no other means of earning money or of receiving support from families. Although the list of help given is long, it is possible to see through the records to the misery and desperation of daily life for the many who struggled to feed and clothe themselves.

Certain names crop up regularly in the records. The 1633 accounts show several payments to Old Blynd Lowell. In February, 'three ells of cloth for a shyrt he having nott wherewith to shift him', in March, 'towards paying of his half year's rent at our Lady Day'. In April he received six pence, in June only four pence and in October, when he was 'in Grett want', one shilling. Alice Cofeld,

In November 1724, *An Account of Several Work-Houses* reported of Peterborough that:

The Number of the aged poor People now in this workhouse is 30. Those that are able, employ'd in Knitting.

The Number of Children is 19. Those that are able, employ'd in Spinning. 49 In all.

	l. s. d.
The Expence for maintaining the House from Lady-Day 1724, to Michaelmas following, in Victuals and Drink, including Apparel and Bedding	159 05 05½
The Product of the Labour of the Poor at the same Time	10 15 03¾
Out of Purse	148 10 01¾

Their Weekly Bill of Fare is much the same as in other Places.

The Savings to the Parish out of the former Charge for maintaining the Poor, will best appear by the following Account.

	l. s. d.
The last 8 Years Charge, one with another, was,	499 18 06¼
But the first half Year, since the Erecting the House of Maintenance, buying of Furniture, Brewing-Vessels, Cloathing, and Repairs, amounts to	220 13 05¾
The last half Year, since Lady-Day, amounts to	113 14 06¾

This information would have related to the parish workhouse run by the feoffees. In the late eighteenth century there would have been over 100 people being housed in the workhouse here. Some of the inmates, especially children, might also be sent out to work in the fields when farmers needed extra help. However, much of the poor relief was provided to the needy outside the workhouse, a situation which continued even after the new Poor Laws of 1834.

'Wattle and daub' buildings had a frame of woven wooden strips which were then 'daubed' with a wet mixture of mud or clay and possibly animal dung and straw.

Cumbergate Workhouse.

dehydrate a patient. Although modern medicine can treat cholera, huge numbers of people died in great pain caused by muscle cramps. Death could follow very swiftly from the first signs of sickness. The patient became very cold and pale and they were said to be in a state of living death during the last stages of the illness.

The feoffees were instructed to provide a parish workhouse and work for the inmates. The first keeper of the workhouse in Cumbergate earned £50 a year and was provided with a coat worth fifty shillings.

remains of butchered animals to rot. Dead dogs or pigs might be left for days and householders' pigs wandered round outside. The stench and filth must have been awful, but – even worse – the town's water supply came from open wells which became dirty and infected.

Cholera is common where water and food is contaminated by such things as human waste. When the only source of drinking water was in the same place as the sewerage ditches, there were naturally frequent outbreaks of the disease. Symptoms include severe diarrhoea and sickness which rapidly

Spinning and knitting had been the major source of employment since the Middle Ages when thousands of sheep grazed the common land. The feoffees' records show gifts of wool given by individuals to provide employment for the poor. Appropriately, Cumbergate was the street of the woolcombers and together with Westgate (Webstergate), the street of the wool weavers, formed the heart of the town in the Middle Ages. The Cumbergate Workhouse could not support the numbers of people needing help, and only twenty years after it opened the feoffees sought help in finding another building. MP Edward Wortley gave land and houses in Westgate to increase accommodation.

AD 1500-1800

CRIME AND PUNISHMENT

The Human and Financial Cost of Breaking the Law

IF YOU HAD committed a crime in the Soke of Peterborough, you were taken to the abbot's gaol and court for judgement. For example, a man had to take his corn to be ground at his lord's mill or face a fine, and until the Dissolution of the Monasteries the lord in question would have been the abbot. The right to hold courts and pronounce sentence, even the death sentence, was granted to the abbots of Peterborough over 1,000 years ago. In matters of justice, the Soke was completely independent of Northamptonshire. One of the advantages was that the fines and goods forfeited by a convicted criminal were paid to the abbey – a lucrative source of income.

For those guilty of more serious crimes, the abbot's gaol awaited them until their trial and subsequent punishment. A spell in the stocks in the market place might not be as easy an option as imagined. Serious injuries could result from the things thrown at the offender and some did not survive their punishment. In 1577, the gaol at the cathedral gates became the responsibility of the new lord paramount of the Liberty of Peterborough, the Earl of Exeter of Burghley House.

Causing an obstruction, by leaving carts in the road for example, was a fairly common charge brought before

Burghley, seat of the Earl of Exeter.

Stocks, many examples of which are still extant.

the courts. A more unusual case was that of someone who blocked the street with a boat whilst carrying out repairs. Dunghills, heaps of earth and 'myre', dead dogs and dead pigs, were frequent hazards that had to be negotiated. One man was charged more than once for letting pigs stray in the street after dark instead of putting them back in their pigsties when they had been brought back from foraging on the common land.

A dyer was fined for 'emptying the filth of his vats' outside his premises. Surprisingly, perhaps, considering what else was lying around, a lady was fined two pennies at Michaelmas in 1582 for emptying the contents of a chamber pot outside – though she did throw it from an upstairs window! Many fines were

imposed on people for not keeping drains outside their premises clear. Great and small were equally guilty of this neglect; Bishop Scambler was fined for letting drains and ditches become blocked, as had his predecessors in the abbey before him. All of these cases paint a vivid picture of how open drains and the nearby wells spread diseases such as cholera, as well as increasing the squalor of the busy town centre. Landlords and owners including the dean and chapter were penalised for not maintaining their property. One case was brought for 'failure to build a chimney' and similarly for lighting fires in houses without a chimney.

Even public buildings were not immune; in 1589 there was a fire in the Guild Hall caused by someone prepared to overlook the lack of a hearth and chimney in an effort to warm the place. Perhaps that is one reason why some meetings adjourned to people's houses, or better still, to the nearest inn!

During the sixteenth century, there seems to have been a standard fine for fighting in the street. If blood was drawn, the normal cost to the offender was three shillings and four pence, but a bruise would cost him four pence. It is hard to imagine calculations of cost being made in the middle of an affray but certainly insulting a constable would always cost the offender four pence. At Easter in 1564, a stabbing which (naturally) drew blood cost both the wielder of the knife and the victim three shillings and four pence, as 'both were at fault'. The following Easter someone was lucky not to have drawn blood when he knocked a man on the head with a stone, though on that occasion six pence seemed a more appropriate punishment.

'Scolds' (usually women!) who were constantly abusive and finding fault were punished in some places by being fitted with a 'scold's bridle', otherwise known as a gossip's bridle or a brank. The bridle was a framework fastened over the head, fitted with a metal plate which rested on top of the tongue. Not only did it prevent speech, it was an extremely painful form of torture. Some versions of the scold's bridle had a bell on top to draw even more attention to the wearer, if that were possible. In Peterborough a two pence fine seemed to do the trick and was much more humane.

In 1584, men had to pay the courts for not wearing 'an English woollen cap' when they went to church. A law had been introduced in the 1570s that required every man except nobility to wear this headgear on Sundays. In a town where much wealth and employment came from the woollen industry the resulting trade would have no doubt been very welcome. Traders often fell foul of the law for giving wrong weights or measures of ale, and in 1575 a man was accused of charging an excessive price for candles. There is no mention of what was considered excessive, or of who decided the matter. Not baiting a bull with dogs before slaughter got a butcher into trouble in 1591, but butchers were regularly in trouble for the mess around their stalls on or after market days.

Fen Reeves were responsible for maintaining drains and ditches in the Fens to avert the very real threat of flooding. The court had to deal with four Fen Reeves on a charge of neglecting their duty by allowing the ditch banks to collapse, though one of the four was dead when he was summoned and therefore beyond the punishment of his earthly accusers.

At this period in history, the town was divided into wards. Each ward had a constable whose job was to maintain order. Unlicensed 'tippling houses' were a big problem, as was the encouraging or playing of prohibited games, which included gambling with cards or dice; at one time, even bowls, tennis and quoits were banned. The main reason for prohibiting people from some of these pastimes was that they then failed to practise archery – a requirement

Practising at the archery butts.

A typical fifteenth-century archer.

badges, knee breeches and a cocked hat reflected their important position in the town. It was their job to see that tramps went on their way, to deal with troublemakers and, in 1662, to make sure that people attended church. The beadles also carried a large mace, which must have helped them impose their authority! Beadles were paid by results so were undoubtedly keen to perform their duties. One notable beadle called Cook, quite a small man, was in charge of the lock-up near the cathedral gates. He was in charge of the stocks and was also responsible for whipping offenders 'at the cart's tail'. The prisoner was stripped to the waist, tied to the back of a cart and dragged round the town on his knees whilst being whipped. This medieval punishment was last carried out in Peterborough in 1819 on a man who had been convicted of stealing malt.

Mr Cook's small physical size sometimes made it difficult for him to deal with stronger offenders, much to the amusement of bystanders. On one occasion when he had to take 'a gigantic and powerful navvy' to the lock-up, the prisoner suddenly swung round, picked up the beadle and carried him all the way to the lock-up. One can just imagine Mr Cook's indignation at this affront to his importance, but the report does not suggest that the navvy went so far as to lock him up in his place!

In contrast to the beadle, the two town bailiffs appointed by the feoffees had to collect rents as well as checking the good maintenance of roads, bridges and town wells.

placed on everyone who might be called upon to fight. Public holidays were often supposed to be used for archery and, again, fines were imposed on those who did not go to the town archery butts to shoot at the targets there.

Ale-conners had to test the quality of ale, beer and bread and check that correct measures were being sold. Like the constables and their assistants, each ward had their own ale-conner, probably necessary considering there were so many drinking houses!

In 1911 a local paper recalled the town beadles of earlier days. Their splendid blue uniforms with large silver

The feoffees' House of Correction, or Bridewell, was on the corner of Cumbergate and was the place where those who had committed minor crimes were held and given work to do. As in the other gaol, the beds were planks and the rooms were small and dark. The poor state of both gaols and the danger of escape increased local demand for a new prison. A new gaol was built in 1840 on Thorpe Road, though it ceased to be used for prisoners forty years later. The building became the magistrates' court or Sessions House until the 1980s.

The other town gaol, under the jurisdiction of Lord Burghley, was a notoriously dreadful place, cramped and uncomfortable. There were three stone cells below the entrance to the precincts with no air and light except that which came through the metal grilles in the doors. Beds were planks covered with straw and blankets and there was no form of heating. Prisoners were sometimes chained to the walls but even so, some managed to escape, especially as the condition of the gaol deteriorated over the years. In 1814 Robert Wass was imprisoned for robbing and assaulting a lady in her home. He had released himself from his chains and managed to get into the next-door cell by making a hole in the thick stone wall. From there he was able to escape with the help of an accomplice.

The town gallows were near Boroughbury but were later moved out to Millfield. A condemned man could be sent to Northampton for execution, which became the rule in the nineteenth century, but whilst the gallows remained, a public hanging was a day's outing for many.

DISEASES, REMEDIES AND 'RESURRECTIONS'

Eccentric Residents and Wicked Bodysnatchers

LADY MARY WORTLEY MONTAGU

'Dirty, avaricious, heartless, and eccentric to the point of insanity.'

THESE ARE WORDS of the writer Alexander Pope, written at the end of their alleged affair, part of an ongoing exchange of insults between the writer and the remarkable Lady Mary Wortley Montagu.

A brilliant wit and writer, a well-educated, independent woman who was an early supporter of women's rights, Mary was the daughter of the Earl of Kingston upon Hull. Her father forbade her marriage to Edward Wortley Montagu, later MP for Peterborough, so the couple eloped. When her husband became ambassador to Turkey, she travelled with him, immersing herself in local history and culture. Having recovered from smallpox, which had left her beauty scarred, she became interested in the Turkish method of inoculation against the disease. Her own child was inoculated although the practice was not without risk.

On returning to England, she used her contacts at court to persuade the Princess of Wales to have her own children inoculated. Four prisoners under sentence of death were selected to be 'guinea pigs' in return for escaping execution. The experiment was successful and Lady Mary carried on her campaign to spread this method of protection against the disease. She brought two doctors to Peterborough to begin inoculating the local population. Unfortunately, however, Peterborough was not ready to submit itself to the ideas of this strange and rather eccentric woman and the inoculators were forced to flee. It would be over seventy years before the safer method of vaccination would be developed by Edward Jenner.

It was her husband, Edward Wortley Montagu, who established the Wortley

Turkish house of Lady Montagu. (Courtesy of Travelers in the Middle East Archive, TIMEA)

Almshouses in Westgate, Peterborough. This building later became a workhouse and today is a public house.

BURIALS AND BODYSNATCHERS

Advances in medicine and increasing numbers of those training to become doctors and surgeons led to the need for more bodies for dissection than were available from traditional sources. Religious scruples at the time led people to believe that the bodies of the dead must not be interfered with in order to ensure their resurrection from the dead at the Last Judgement. Until 1832, when the Anatomy Act was passed, only executed criminals or the unclaimed bodies of paupers could be used by the medical profession for research purposes. Demand for more bodies led directly to the gruesome crime of bodysnatching. There was a ready market and good money for anyone supplying a corpse, provided that it was made available soon after burial. The people who carried out these crimes were known as Resurrection Men. No cemetery was safe from them and watchmen were appointed to prevent a grave being dug up after a funeral. The most notorious bodysnatchers of their day were Burke and Hare from Edinburgh, who actually resorted to murder in order to keep up the supply of 'fresh' bodies.

One local case in 1830 reveals the rewards that tempted people to get involved in the macabre business of grave robbing. Two labourers, Whayley and Patrick, were charged with stealing a body from Yaxley churchyard at the instigation of a Mr Grimmer. Grimmer had repeatedly offered Patrick money for corpses and he in turn offered Whayley half a sovereign. Several witnesses implicated Patrick, who boasted about how the watchman had never seen him taking sacks of bodies to Peterborough, especially when a bit of money changed hands to ensure he turned a blind eye to the proceedings. Someone else testified that he had gone with Grimmer and another man to move a corpse found in 'Doctor Johnson's hovel' in Peterborough. This seems to tie in with the story of a man sleeping off the effects of a night's drinking in the shed of a doctor and then waking to find he was lying on a sack containing the body of a woman called Mrs Biggins who had been recently buried. The doctor was not implicated in any crime but someone who had been staying at his house reportedly made a hasty departure for London. Perhaps he was just squeamish?

It was some time later that the gravedigger, who suddenly had plenty of money at his disposal, was accused of the crime. A newspaper report from 1911 points out that there had been rival gangs of Resurrection Men operating in Peterborough at the time and that those who had dug up Mrs Biggins had fled the scene, only to have a second gang come and steal the sack containing her body.

The Peterborough cemetery at the time was at the top of Cowgate, near the town centre. When the new cemetery came into use some people anticipated that its location would attract bodysnatchers. Mr Bower, the ironmonger, was the first person to be interred there and watchmen were paid to guard the grave 'for weeks' after his funeral. Previously the cemetery had been located on the north side of the cathedral. Although there was no known cemetery associated with the parish church of St John, recent work in the town square uncovered several graves laid out in an orderly fashion.

A book published in 1905 mentions the tombstone on a girl's grave found at a crossroads near Boroughbury. Originally sited outside the town near the abbey's Tithe Barn, only fields surrounded the place where the four roads met. The girl had been buried with a stake through the body and obviously outside consecrated ground. It was not until 1823 that the bodies of those who had committed suicide were generally allowed to be buried in public cemeteries or in the consecrated area of a church graveyard. In earlier times, suicides and the corpses of those found guilty of violent crimes were often buried by the side of roads or in the middle of crossroads outside of towns.

Sometimes bodies were placed in the ground face down or with stakes through them, supposedly to stop the dead rising again. Apparently the girl's grave marked such a site, though it seems a tombstone had been placed there at some point.

AD 1790

NORMAN CROSS

The World's First Purpose-Built Prisoner-of-War Camp

DURING THE NAPOLEONIC Wars of the late eighteenth to early nineteenth centuries, thousands of prisoners were taken from captured ships and became the responsibility of the Royal Navy. Some were kept overseas where they had been captured, whilst others were held aboard prison ships. When all available prisons were full, it was decided to build a new prison, far enough from the sea to make escape from England difficult, but close enough to somewhere that could supply the needs of captives and their guards. The site chosen was next to the Great North Road, at a place which became known as Norman Cross in Peterborough.

The first intake arrived in April 1797 and between then and its closure in June 1814, thousands of prisoners passed through the camp's gates. An average of something over 5,000 inmates were held at any one time. The prison was divided into four quadrangles and prisoners spent all day out of doors unless the weather was very bad. Each quadrangle was visited by a doctor every day; prisoners who complained of being ill were examined and sent to the camp hospital if necessary.

Locally sourced fresh food was provided firstly by the British Government, then, under a reciprocal arrangement for prisoners of war, by the French. Typical rations included fresh meat and vegetables, bread, cheese and beer in sufficient quantities to provide a basic healthy diet. Patients received more whilst they were being treated in the prison hospital. In addition, each person was provided with a mattress stuffed with straw or sawdust, two blankets and a thin pillow. Bright yellow trousers and jackets and red waistcoats were provided, designed to make sure no one who escaped could fail to be noticed! These provisions did not stop some suffering from starvation or cold due to the obsession with gambling, one of the major problems at Norman Cross. Owning nothing but the clothes they stood up in and their bedding, some prisoners gambled away their rations and were known to fight over piles of rubbish and potato peelings in their search for food. Their clothes and bedding went the way of their food and large numbers were left in rags, hungry and vulnerable to illness.

Large numbers of people in confined quarters meant that disease spread quickly. There were cases of pneumonia and consumption but most deaths occurred during a typhus epidemic in 1800 to 1801. The hospital and medical staff could not cope and many inmates were left to die in their beds. A special cemetery had to be built outside the camp's perimeter in order to bury over 1,000 victims. During the seventeen years Norman Cross was open it is estimated that about 1,700 people died during their imprisonment.

Napoleon and his soldiers, many of whom were captured and ended up in Peterborough's prisoner-of-war camp. (LC-DIG-pga-04089)

Most breaches of discipline were punished by the offender's rations being reduced. More serious offences, such as attacking a guard, meant a spell in the 'Black Hole', a cell block without windows where the prisoner would be chained to restrict his movement. Privileges, such as being included in any exchange whereby English prisoners would be returned in exchange for French ones, were removed. Local courts heard cases such as forgery of banknotes and other assault cases. Only one prisoner was sentenced to death by the court – he had stabbed a local man during a failed escape attempt. His death by hanging was carried out at Norman Cross, in front of the other prisoners. One French officer was killed when he made a bid for freedom from the Angel Inn in Peterborough where he was being held temporarily before being moved to the prison.

More than 700 daggers were found during one search and fights between inmates were common. There were frequent escape attempts but most prisoners did not get far before they were recaptured or shot. Usually quite small numbers were involved, but on one occasion in 1807 about 500 men managed to break down some of the wooden barriers in the prison. The guards drove them back with bayonets, wounding at least forty in the process. Following this incident, wooden barriers were replaced by solid walls.

On a more positive note, prisoners were taught to read and write, and those who could read had access to books. They were

French Eagle memorial at Norman Cross.

fire engine! Beautiful marquetry boxes and intricately carved models such as toys, ships and even a guillotine were produced, and some prisoners were able to earn large sums of money, especially when commissioned to make a special article for a local customer. Split straw was also braided into plaits which were sold for hat and basket making. Large amounts of money could be made selling straw plaits: traders were happy to buy from the prisoners and avoid the tax they should have been paying. Although the trade was illegal, the rewards were so high that it continued despite the risks. A sergeant in the militia stationed at Norman Cross, who had supposedly tried to stop the smuggling of straw plaits, was attacked near the camp by a group of men. He was robbed and then a piece of his tongue was cut off, possibly as punishment for his opposition to the trade.

allowed to make goods for sale at public markets and used readily available straw to make baskets and hats. This conflicted with local trade so they turned to making models out of straw and animal bone. Their earnings allowed them to purchase more materials and examples of their wonderful craftsmanship are on display at Peterborough Museum. You can also see the tools used and even the camp

When Norman Cross was closed down in 1814, at the end of the war against Napoleon, several prisoners remained in the area. Most of the buildings were knocked down and the building materials sold on. A memorial to those who died at the prison was later erected at the site.

AD 1750-1850

SMELLY STREETS AND HORNED ANIMALS

Terrible True Stories of Transport

CITY STREETS WERE notorious for being badly maintained, muddy and frequently flooded. Ladies especially were unwilling to walk through the dirt and found other modes of transport. Sedan chairs were still being used in Peterborough in the late 1860s, long after most places had got rid of them. They were carried on poles by two men and the charge was one shilling or one shilling and sixpence on nights when there was a ball. Some of those who carried the chairs were said to be rude and sometimes drunk but passengers did not always pay a fair amount for their journey. A 'Committee for the Management of Sedan Chairs' was set up and in 1798 Mr Henry Walker of Westgate was chosen to take charge of the service.

Carriages did not always prove to be a better option. A report in the local paper tells of one incident when two ladies were returning home from a ball in all their finery, wearing evening dresses and silk slippers. They took a carriage, hoping to avoid damage to their clothes from the dirty roads. Not long after they began their journey home, the floor of their carriage fell off – unnoticed by the coachman, who failed to hear the ladies' cries for help. Their feet were touching the ground and they were forced to run along inside the carriage until they finally caught the attention of their driver! The report adds that they were fortunate because the horse was well-behaved. One wonders whether the coachman was made to pay for the damage to their lovely evening slippers and gowns.

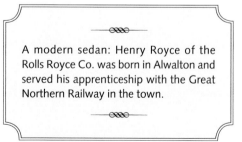

A modern sedan: Henry Royce of the Rolls Royce Co. was born in Alwalton and served his apprenticeship with the Great Northern Railway in the town.

Satirical cartoon showing George VI riding in a sedan chair, popular in Peterborough, whilst Queen Caroline rides on top. (LC-USZ62-85550)

In the late nineteenth century the cattle market was close to Long Causeway, and local hotels and inns which provided accommodation for people going to market also used outbuildings to house some of their animals. Animals were led through town to the market and ladies were apparently prevented from shopping because they had to walk along the dirty streets. A writer commented that:

> The female mind abhors anything approaching contact with horned animals. It takes the pleasure out of shopping if she thought she might meet a restless-looking cow, or a doubtful looking ox and takes away all notion of colour,

shape, and measure, or whether the thing will wash or not. Long Causeway was therefore practically abandoned on market days, and not much more used on other days for shopping purposes, because on anything like changeable or damp weather the atmosphere of the street was what I have heard ladies describe (not meaning to be complimentary) as 'smelly'.

Horse-drawn buses ran from the mid-nineteenth century and cannot have improved the cleanliness of the streets. By the beginning of the twentieth century horse-drawn buses had been replaced by electric trams, which ran until motor buses took over transport services in the 1930s.

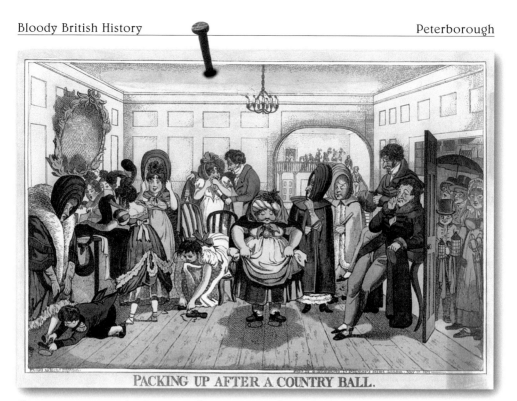

PACKING UP AFTER A COUNTRY BALL.

Contemporary cartoon showing women dressing to return home after a country ball . (LC-USZ62-85550)

Goods and passengers travelling to or from the city used coaches or river transport until the arrival of railways in the middle of the nineteenth century. A passenger boat went regularly to and from Wisbech, and goods were transported by barge as they had been from the earliest times. There was a river port on the Nene in Saxon times and stone used in building the abbey had arrived by barge from the quarries at Barnack. The Toll House, or Customs House, near the town bridge, was where barges passing up or down the river had to pay tolls or taxes on goods. Cargoes included agricultural produce, barley (which provided malt for brewing), wood and stone. The little lantern tower on top of the eighteenth-century building probably had a light to guide river traffic.

French prisoners captured during the Napoleonic Wars were brought here by boat and then marched out to Norman Cross prisoner-of-war camp.

Many men worked on the river and 'waterman' is frequently given as the regular job of those in the local militia. Workers and their families lived by the river in 'yards', groups of dwellings around a yard where a single pump provided water for everyone living there. Overcrowding was common, sanitation poor and flooding made life more difficult before the Nene Embankment helped to contain the water levels. Although the houses there have gone, the name 'Hill's

Legends of the Fens

THE MYTH OF the Wild Hunt is known throughout Europe, and the appearance of the ghostly hunters always foretold disaster and death. In some cases those who witnessed it were condemned to die so that their souls could join the demons in the sky as they swept past. The Wild Hunt was described by the monks of Peterborough Abbey at the beginning of the twelfth century when Henry I appointed Henry de Poitou, also known as Henry d'Angely, as abbot. Henry d'Angely was known to be corrupt and have two abbeys under his control. His arrival was seen as a curse on the abbey and the town and this was confirmed by the appearance of the phantom huntsmen. For nine weeks the Wild Hunt was seen riding in the sky from Stamford to Peterborough, through the town's deer park to the very walls of the abbey. About thirty people, including the monks themselves, are said to have heard the horns and the terrifying howls of the hounds as they tore through the night skies. The huntsmen rode large black horses and goats, horrible to behold as they followed their hell hounds, eyes the size of saucers burning fire, through the darkness. It was said that the hunters were the cursed souls of the dead, whilst the descriptions of their dogs recalled the ghostly dogs said to haunt the area.

BLACK SHUCK, HELL HOUND

Did the ghostly tales of Black Shuck inspire Sir Arthur Conan Doyle to write the Sherlock Holmes story *The Hound of the Baskervilles*, the tale of a demonic dog that seems to haunt the Baskerville family and lead men to their death? The Old English word 'scucca' means demon and, like the Wild Hunt, the Shuck was thought to bring death or madness to those who encountered it. The shaggy black dog with red flaming eyes is rumoured to roam the countryside around Peterborough and the Fenlands.

The hell hounds strike! (LC-USZC4-1298)

Legends say that it appears in a swirling cloud of mists or lurks on the edge of your vision. Strangely, others said that it was a benign spirit which came to guide those who were lost. They merely had to follow it to safety. The choice was yours...

WILL-O'-THE –WISP

Gases rising from the marshes can sometimes burst into flame as they bubble up and meet the air. This phenomenon no doubt gave rise to descriptions of evil spirits and ghostly creatures lurking beneath the murky waters of the Fens. In the early part of the eighth century, Guthlac, a Mercian nobleman, chose to devote himself to a life of religious contemplation and sought out the isolated island of Croyland (now Crowland). His meagre diet and the unhealthy environment weakened his health. He saw demons rising out of the mists blowing tongues of flame into the air and seeming to gabble in Welsh! The mists in this area create a mysterious and eerie landscape where people feared that the little flames were spirits of the dead who had drowned. The flickering lights were called will-o'-the-wisps, who summoned lost travellers away from safe paths to watery deaths.

LANTERN MEN

Lantern men were even more to be dreaded than will-o'-the-wisps, appearing in the twisted shape of a man holding a lantern, beckoning the unwary to follow their light. Once they had their victim, they held them under the water until they drowned or simply devoured them. Those who whistled to bolster their courage as they picked their way through

THE BONES OF NORMAN SOLDIERS

When Hereward escaped the Norman soldiers who were pursuing him, he set fire to the causeway they had constructed to reach his hideout. The causeway collapsed and the Normans fell into the dark waters below. Unable to help themselves because of the weight of their armour, they drowned. Years later, people claim to have pulled up the skeletons of those who had lain for centuries held by the mud and the reeds.

the high reeds and bogs were always taken by the Lantern Men. The sound of whistling called them up and drew them to their prey, who was never seen again. The one hope of survival was to lie face down on the ground and hold your breath until the dreadful apparitions floated away.

GHOSTS OF LOST ROMAN SOLDIERS

During the Roman occupation of Britain the little areas of higher ground that rose above the waters of the Fens became lonely outposts for soldiers guarding the frontiers of their territory from hostile local tribes. A soldier who lost his way would be in danger of drowning if he strayed off the path and the ghosts of those dead soldiers are said to haunt the marshes still.

Peterborough Cathedral from the south: Canute's two sons were drowned as they headed for the city. (LC-DIG-ppmsc-08782)

CANUTE (KNUT)

It was believed that the Danish ruler of England, Canute, ordered the building of a dyke along the edge of the Mere at Ramsey, the area now known as King's Delph. Whilst visiting his hunting lodge at Bodsey Island, he and his companions set out to sail to Peterborough across the Mere. Two of his sons drowned when a violent storm caused their boat to capsize. The dyke was built to provide a safe alternative route for future travellers.

LOST IN THE FENS!

Not all those who were lost in the Fens were overcome by the powers of the supernatural! The fortunate escape of one Peterborough man continues to be remembered in the city to this day.

Every year on 15 March the bells of St John's parish church in Cathedral Square ring out the Wyldebore peal, a tradition that dates back to the eighteenth century. Matthew Wyldbore became one of Peterborough's MPs and lived in the Mansion House in Westgate, near the site of the Bull Hotel. Whilst out riding one day, he became lost in the thick mists that rise from the Fens. The dangers of leaving the right path and drowning were well known to locals so Matthew Wyldebore was relieved to hear the bells of St John's ringing and guiding him to safety. When he died in 1781 he still remembered the debt he owed to the bell-ringers of St John's and in gratitude he left enough money to pay for bells to be rung every year on 15 March, the anniversary of his birth – and his death. Although the amount paid to the bell-ringers has varied since the original bequest, the Wyldebore peal is still rung every year. In addition to the ringing of the bells, he requested that a sermon be preached on the same day. This has not happened since 1995.

In 1774 he was elected MP for the second time. His will also remembered all who had voted for him and had attended his funeral!

SEVERED HEADS AND STOLEN TREASURES: THE LEGEND OF HEREWARD THE WAKE

Hereward's fight against William the Conqueror after the Norman invasion of England in 1066 made him into a symbol of English resistance, a legendary leader whose exploits were written about long after his death. Like the later folk hero Robin Hood, it is hard to separate fact from fiction, especially in the absence of much evidence from the documents written at the time. Charles Kingsley,

Ely, where Hereward launched his invasion. (LC-DIG-ppmsc-08362)

Hereward the Wake.

who lived in the parish of Barnack, turned the little known facts about the local Saxon legend into a romantic tale of an English hero.

He told the story of Hereward fighting a great white bear when he was travelling in Northumbria after leaving home. The savage bear was part of a menagerie of wild animals kept by his host. One day the bear escaped, attacking dogs and a horse while the members of the household cowered in fear behind locked doors. A small child had been locked outside and as the bear turned towards her Hereward leapt from his horse, raised his sword and struck the bear's head with such force that it died instantly. Kingsley's next story of Hereward's prowess in combat tells how he defeated Ironhook, a giant of a Cornishman, to save a princess from his cruelty. It was the princess who stole Ironhook's sword Brainbiter, which Hereward took for his own.

Hereward's family had a manor at Bourne in Lincolnshire and possibly also held land for the abbey of Peterborough. As he grew up, Hereward gained a reputation as a troublemaker who defied authority to such an extent that his own father, Leofric, asked the King to banish him. He travelled to Flanders where he learnt the art of warfare fighting as a mercenary and winning a reputation as a great soldier. After the defeat of King Harold at the Battle of Hastings, Hereward returned to England where the Saxon English were trying to drive out the Normans. He returned home to find that the family's lands had been taken over by the invaders but even worse was the horrific sight that awaited him at his home. The head of his brother had been hung above the door of the house as a symbol of Norman supremacy. Hereward set out to exact a terrible revenge on his brother's killers and slaughtered them single-handedly, killing over a dozen men and beheading them with his sword, Brainbiter. Their heads replaced the head of his brother, sending out a bloody warning that other Normans would meet the same fate. He fled to the relative safety of the Fens where only those who knew the safe paths through the marshes could be sure of survival, intent on leading a fierce resistance against the enemy. Local people rallied to his cause and he became a leader of the rebellion against William the Conqueror.

In 1170 Hereward joined forces with a Danish army sent to fight against the Normans. The Danes based themselves on the Isle of Ely from where they launched an attack on the great abbey of Peterborough, now under the control of a Norman abbot, Turold. Hereward claimed he wanted to take the abbey's treasure to ensure it did not fall into Turold's hands and one version of the story says that some believed him because he was 'a man of the monks'. As the treasure was supposedly divided between the Danes and Hereward's men, it does not seem likely that it would have found its way back to the abbey. Turold was still in Stamford when Hereward and his allies arrived in their boats early in the morning, having sailed through the waters of the Fens right up to the walls of the abbey. The ensuing battle was brutal and despite the best efforts of the monks

The great white bear which fought Hereward was probably a polar bear; it had escaped from a nearby menagerie.

A spectral hunt once haunted the skies above Peterborough.

with them. They did not all live to enjoy their wealth as dreadful storms sank some of their laden ships.

Hereward was now seen as a major threat to Norman rule and William determined to capture him. The problems of actually engaging Hereward in battle were immense – the Fens provided a safe haven for the rebels and without local help, no Norman army could reach him. Hereward was able to launch guerrilla style attacks on the Normans with no fear of reprisal. The Normans, meanwhile, were making plans to cross the Fens by building a long wooden causeway through the marshes to enable their soldiers to reach Hereward's base. Using a disguise to infiltrate the Norman camp, Hereward overheard their plans and he and his men hid in the reeds by the causeway until William's men were marching across it. It was an easy matter for the Saxons to set fire to the wooden pathway, and it collapsed under the weight of the soldiers, throwing them to their death in the waters below, unable to save themselves because of the weight of their armour.

The end came when Hereward was betrayed by someone who knew the safe paths across the Fens and led William's army to their enemy. Did Hereward die in the fight that followed, or did he escape yet again? Some versions of the legend say that he made peace with William, but others tell that he fought to the death. Whether or not a real Hereward – rebellious youth, fearless swordsman and inspirational leader – died in a last battle in the Fens, his name lives on locally as a heroic figure who bravely resisted his enemies.

to defend themselves and the Church's treasures, Hereward and his men escaped with gold and silver as well as relics. Some monks were also taken with the soldiers back to their stronghold, leaving the town and monastery buildings burning and the remaining monks fleeing to safety. The Fenland base was secure, and the Normans could not follow them to their hideout. However, the pause in hostilities did not last long, and Hereward had to retreat into the deeper Fens again. The Danes made peace with William and went back to Denmark, taking most of the plunder

Yard' can be seen near the entrance to the Rivergate Centre to remind people of the time when working on the Nene or in the warehouses there was a major source of employment.

RAILWAY TOWN

In the early nineteenth century there were about 4,000 people living in the market town of Peterborough. The majority of the working population were employed on the land or on the river. River transport carried grain from the farmlands to the east of the town, and stone and timber from the higher country to the west. There were breweries and small-scale brick making, which was carried on at various clay pits around the town. Clay pipes, baskets and hats were made locally but it was only in 1830 that heavier industry started to appear in Peterborough with the opening of a small iron foundry.

Only a few years later, the slow pace of life in the town would change forever. The location of Peterborough made it attractive to the new railway companies and workers rushed to take up opportunities offered by the new industry. The transformation from market town to industrial town took only a few years but initially the countryside to the south of the town caused the railway engineers problems. In the seventeenth century major engineering work had transformed the watery Fenlands into rich agricultural land by means of extensive drainage systems. As the railway approached Peterborough, a way had to be found to cross the marshy land, and the solution was found by a young engineer with experience of working on the Fen drainage system. Thomas Brassey and his agent, Stephen Ballard, arranged for rafts of wood and layers of peat to be sunk into the ground to form a firm foundation for the tracks. Brassey's cast-iron bridge, built to carry the railway over the River Nene in Peterborough, is still in use today.

The town started to spread out along the line of tracks as workshops and workers' cottages were built. Not only houses but schools and churches were provided by the railway companies for their employees. Work was hard and could be dangerous. Men were killed in explosions in the marshalling yards where trains were taken for maintenance and repair, and there were accidents on the tracks and at level crossings. The Crescent Crossing was particularly dangerous, and it was finally replaced by a bridge after a woman was killed there. Peterborough's brick production soared thanks to new developments in the industry and local companies were able to transport millions of bricks more cheaply and easily thanks to the railways. Peterborough became a major centre for engineering and continued to grow throughout the next century.

AD 1800

THE PEASANT POET

John Clare, a Troubled Genius

JOHN CLARE, THE 'Peasant Poet', spent the last twenty-three years of his life in the Northampton General Lunatic Asylum. He had been under the care of Fenwick Skrimshire, who had been physician at the Peterborough Public Dispensary for twenty years, but Clare's increasingly erratic and violent behaviour meant that his wife could no longer take care of him. It was Dr Skrimshire who signed the papers committing him to the asylum. In answer to the question, 'Was the insanity preceded by any severe or long-continued mental emotion or exertion?', Dr Skrimshire entered 'years of poetical prosing'.

Here he lived out his days, encouraged to write poetry by the doctor there. 'I am', one of his best-known poems, tells of the isolation he felt because of his mental condition and his hopes of returning to his beloved countryside.

John Clare was born in the Soke of Peterborough, in the village of Helpston, in 1793. He received limited schooling until he was twelve years old. At the school, which was held in the church of Glinton village, he met the girl who was to inspire him throughout his life. Mary Joyce was the daughter of a successful farmer who would not allow the relationship to continue. Clare tried several jobs, such as working for the local pub landlord, gardening, the militia and lime burning, but it was mainly as an agricultural worker that he made his living.

He had been able to borrow books and loved reading. His mother told him folk tales and his father played the fiddle and particularly loved singing local ballads. Clare was so inspired by a book of poetry called *Seasons* by James Thompson that he left his work at the local public house to another boy and walked all the way to Stamford to buy it. This was the turning point in his life. He began to write about the countryside he loved so much, describing village customs and characters but mainly, the birds, insects, animals and flowers. Not having money for writing materials meant that he would scribble his ideas and verses on any available paper using homemade ink. This has made much of his work difficult to read, as editors have tried to piece together poems mixed in with details of household bills or mathematical calculations.

When he was able to buy a blank book of paper for his poems, a local bookseller helped him to find a way to publish it in 1820, the year he married Patty Turner. *Poems Descriptive of Rural Life and Scenery* was an immediate success and made him a celebrity amongst the literary classes. The cottage at Helpston became a place of pilgrimage for those who were fascinated by the 'peasant poet'. Clare would sometimes send his wife to deal with visitors and keep out of the way himself until they had gone.

Amongst those who went to see Clare was the Bishop of Peterborough and his wife. Bishop Marsh and his wife remained friendly with the poet and some years later offered him a room in the Bishop's Palace in Peterborough where he could go and write quietly. They supplied him with paper and inks, but it seems he could never settle to work in the cold room. In 1830 came an event which revealed Clare's deteriorating mental state. He had been invited to accompany the bishop to see a performance of *The Merchant of Venice* at the theatre in Peterborough. As the play progressed, Clare became more agitated. Eventually, he tried to climb out of the bishop's box to attack the character of Shylock.

John Clare's birthplace in Helpston; as a boy, he worked in the Bluebell Inn next door. The village church is at the end of the road.

Unable to distinguish between the acting and reality, he determined to punish the 'villain' of the piece.

Any small profit Clare made from his writing was soon gone, although he did acquire some wealthy patrons including the Earl of Exeter and Lord Fitzwilliam. Later publications did not do as well as literary fashions changed. He always needed money to support himself and his growing family. He returned to working on the land. His health had never been good and, combined with a drinking problem and depression, it rapidly deteriorated. His life was torn between his London literary connections and his home in Helpston. He was sent to an asylum in Essex where it was hoped that constant care and the open-air lifestyle offered there would improve his health.

As his mind failed he began to believe that he was married to Mary Joyce and determined to leave the asylum in Essex

Clare's grave in St Botolph's churchyard, Helpston, reads: 'A poet is born, not made'.

for so long.

During his lifetime, Clare witnessed a period of great change in the countryside which gave rise to his love of poetry. The landscape itself underwent a transformation. Open heath and common land had traditionally been used by everyone as a source of food, wood for fuel and pasture for animals. The freedom to wander wherever he wanted was at the heart of Clare's love of the open spaces round Helpston. He always befriended gypsies who represented that feeling of freedom and originally planned to travel back home with a gypsy family he had met in Essex. Whilst he was still in his home village, the enclosure of the common heaths had begun. Seeking to farm the land more efficiently, landowners began to fence off areas for ploughing, building roads to make access easier and diverting water from some of the old streams.

Driven by necessity, Clare himself had to take work putting up fences, which caused him great pain. He even witnessed surveyors close to the village, working a route for a new railway. Clare never used a train in his lifetime as he travelled by coach, on foot or by boat. As a young man, he had gone from Peterborough to Wisbech in search of a job. Ironically, his first train journey was the one he made after death, from Northampton back to the village where his life began. His gravestone says simply 'A poet is born, not made.'

to see her. He walked for four days, reduced to eating grass to keep him going, and arrived back in Peterborough – to be met by his wife in Walton. Once home he would walk over to the place he used to meet Mary Joyce, tormented by the sight of Glinton church spire across the fields from his cottage in Northborough. He was convinced he would see her again, not accepting that she had died years earlier. His moods became darker and he became more violent. The decision was made to move him to the asylum in Northampton, where he lived as a private patient. He became a familiar sight in the town as he strolled or sat on a bench in the sun outside the asylum. When he died in 1864 his body was taken for burial in the churchyard at Helpston, the village that had been the centre of his life

AD 1834

THE POOR LAW UNION

Destitution, Deprivation and Despair

THE NEW POOR Law was passed in 1834 and replaced that which had been in place since the time of Elizabeth I. The huge increase in those needing help from the parish meant that some areas struggled to meet the cost of providing for them. Town populations were increasing as people left their homes in the countryside and sought work in the new industries springing up in urban centres. Having to bear the financial burden of supporting those who relied on their charity, many people began to resent the expense – and in the Victorian Age, many believed that poor people should be encouraged to help themselves. Parishes were to be grouped together and would share common workhouses which would provide accommodation and work.

Reflecting the social thinking of the time, the 'idle poor' were responsible for their own condition and must work to get themselves out of their situation. It was up to people who needed help to apply for admission and then to leave when they had work. Conditions were to be such that inmates would be discouraged from staying, being deliberately less comfortable than the average workers' accommodation. The new Poor Law Union Workhouses were to be run by a local Board of Guardians. The Board of Guardians in Peterborough was set up in 1835 and they set about finding appropriate premises.

The existing institutions run by the feoffees were unsuitable as they could not be adapted to fulfil the new requirements, such as separate accommodation for men and women. The feoffees themselves were not prepared to give up control of the premises they already ran. A new Union Workhouse was built in Thorpe Road under the direction of a master and his wife, who acted as matron. Other members of staff included a porter and later two teachers for the children. An infirmary building and a chapel were eventually added to the buildings there.

Union workhouse, Thorpe Road.

The obvious problems of being in the workhouse and yet needing to find work sometimes meant that a parent might leave their children and check themselves out whilst they sought employment, then check themselves back in again. The process of asking for admission to the workhouse was humiliating from the first moment and had to be repeated every time someone went back. On entry, individuals were stripped of their own clothes, washed, checked for any signs of infectious diseases and provided with workhouse clothes. They were assigned a diet which was supposed to reflect each one's needs.

1. Able Bodied Men
2. Old and Infirm Men
3. Boys from 9 to 13 or 16
4. Boys from 2 to 9
5. Able Bodied Women
6. Old and Infirm Women
7. Girls from 9 to 13 or 16
8. Girls from 2 to 9
9. Infants

Once their food allocation was decided, each person's diet number was attached to their clothes. Families were separated, men and women being kept in different parts of the building, and children taken away from their parents, who were assumed to have given up care when they went into the workhouse. Children were supposed to receive some education.

The new Union Workhouse register of admission and discharge shows that the majority of adults gave their normal employment as agricultural worker, showing that Peterborough was moving slowly away from agricultural market town to industrial town. However, the box asking whether or not a pauper was able-bodied was ticked more often 'no' than 'yes'. Reason for entry was usually 'destitute', whilst the causes were repeated over and over again: 'old age', 'infirm', 'blind', 'infirm mind', 'infancy', 'paralysed', 'subject to fits', 'orphaned' – in the case of children with only poor relations unable to care for them – or 'abandoned'. Unmarried girls who became pregnant often had nowhere to go but the workhouse.

Thomas Stephenson, aged eleven, from Castor and his brothers James, aged eight, and Joseph, aged five, were abandoned to the workhouse in 1840, and Sarah and William Sexton, aged ten and eight, were orphaned in 1841. Although it is recorded that Sarah had physical disabilities, she absconded in 1841 but later returned to the workhouse. In the case of William Joppis, aged eight, his father had been transported after being convicted of a crime. As they grew older, boys were sent out to a variety of employment. Some were apprenticed to local craftsmen, such as a shoemaker or a whip-maker, whilst girls would usually go out into service.

People living in poverty and struggling to feed and clothe themselves were ill-equipped, or completely unable, to meet the needs of those who were physically or mentally disabled. More and more of those taken into the Union Workhouse were never going to be able to work to support themselves. Staff had only one way of dealing with inmates who had fits or whose mental illness resulted in violence, and that was to physically restrain them, usually by tying them to their beds with towels. The medical officer would be called upon to sign an order for the detention of 'lunatics' in the workhouse and make a report on their condition. Signs of depression or age-related disabilities that would be recognised today were not easily dealt with in the nineteenth century and earlier. Details of those appearing before the medical officer reveal the range of problems: a sixteen-year-old girl was committed to an asylum because she was 'strange in her ways' and could not learn; another could not keep herself clean and laughed or cried without reason; an elderly man whose wife had just died was often confused. The workhouse, of course, was not the right place for them, and the reports make for difficult reading.

RAW MEAT AND KNUCKLE BONES

Old Wives' Tales and a Real 'Florence Nightingale'

WHEN THE NAPOLEONIC Wars ended and the prisoner-of-war camp at Norman Cross was closed, the Peterborough Yeomanry cavalry gave the funds they no longer needed to set up a public dispensary in Peterborough. The dispensary opened in 1821 in Cowgate and had a resident doctor, Dr Pope, a physician, Dr Fenwick Skrimshire, and a visiting surgeon, Thomas Walker. Sick people could not just turn up at the door and hope to be treated. A letter of recommendation from one of the board of governors needed to be handed over by the patient, which restricted the numbers eligible for health care. The infirmary relied on donations and when churches began to raise money through their collections, the clergyman would receive a letter of recommendation for one patient or for two if more than £5 was raised. Other groups, such as workers' organisations, contributed money and received the same privileges.

In the event of a person being too ill to get to the dispensary, no home visits were made unless the patient lived within the minster precincts or in an area administered by the Improvement Commissioners. Paupers were not allowed to use its services unless specifically sent by a parish doctor.

In 1822 further facilities were opened in Milton Street to enable patients to stay if they needed more treatment, but they had to pay for their own upkeep, including food. It was 1840 before a Poor Law infirmary opened for residents of the workhouses. In 1856 Earl Fitzwilliam gave his town house in Priestgate to be used as a hospital, run by the surgeon Thomas Walker. It was thirty years before an operating theatre and an out-patients' section was added. Until then operations had been carried out in the patient's bed at the infirmary, or in their own home. Even worse, until 1847 no anaesthetics were used. In 1865 further extensions were made to the hospital when outbuildings became an isolation unit. Cases of smallpox were still being reported, with three deaths in 1874 and more in 1878. The city needed an isolation hospital to treat diseases such as scarlet fever and diphtheria, but not surprisingly there was strong opposition from residents in places suggested for such a building. Eventually a small unit was built on farmland to the east of the city, at Fengate.

Peterborough was at the forefront of some medical advances, being the first place outside London to use X-rays in 1896. The hospital secretary Alfred Taylor built his own X-ray machine, but in those early days the dangers of radiation poisoning were not known and, sadly, he died as a result of his work.

Through the years when no other medical care was available to the poor, people had relied on local 'wise women' for help in sickness and childbirth. Folklore and superstition were rife in the treatment of illness and the sick put their trust in 'cures' found in almanacs or local custom. As late as 1908 a conversation was recorded between two women on Long Causeway who were discussing a child's whooping cough. The mother had been told by 'Mrs X', probably the local wise woman, to steal a bit of raw meat from the butcher's shop, make a hole in it and put some of her hair inside (usually the child's hair was used). The meat should be fed to a dog and the child would improve. In this case the mother reported that she had done as instructed but the child was no better.

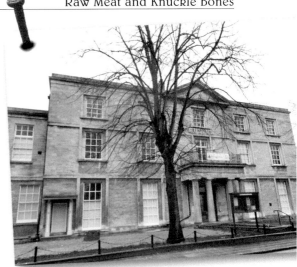

The museum, formerly the infirmary.

A person being treated by a wise woman must believe that they would be cured and not say 'please' or 'thank you' or the cure would not work. A piece of string or leather might be tied round someone's neck after being 'blessed'. The writer noted that many charms are 'used at the present time', that is, the second half of the nineteenth century. There were several superstitions regarding childbirth. When a baby was born the custom was to carry it upstairs so that its prospects in life would rise. If the child was born upstairs the nurse or midwife should pick it up and climb on a chair or put it in a high place to achieve the same results. Some mothers bit their child's nails to keep them short until they were one year old, as cutting them was thought to make the child a thief.

Night cramps could be prevented by placing one's shoes next to the bed in the form of a T; general cramps might be helped by putting a knucklebone in your pocket. To cure ague – a fever – a live spider could be put in a little bag and worn round the neck. Alternatively, it could be swallowed whole, in a paste. If you couldn't face that, then a rolled up woodlouse could be swallowed instead. Carrying a potato, a chestnut or a nutmeg in your pocket was supposed to relieve rheumatism. One of the stranger customs that had been practised was the wearing of a 'fit' ring. Depending on whether it was a man or woman who wanted to cure fits, they should collect nine pieces of silver and nine half pennies from members of the opposite sex. The half pennies would pay a silversmith to make a ring.

Dr Fenwick Scrimshire commented on those who sought help from medically unqualified people in a book for the use of his son, a village clergyman. Stating that professional medical help may not be easily available locally he thought that the vicar might be the right person to ask, being well-educated and trusted. His book is a 'first-aid' manual covering topics as diverse as broken limbs, deep wounds, fits and even different forms of cholera. One can only imagine the amount of time and medical supplies needed to deal with these emergencies – but then, they were for use when there really wasn't an alternative and could possibly mean the difference between life and death. We do not know what medical demands were made on Scrimshire's son, or whether any other local clergyman bought a copy of his book, but hopefully someone was helped.

FLORENCE SAUNDERS: PETERBOROUGH'S 'FLORENCE NIGHTINGALE'

The death of Florence Saunders in 1904 was described in the local newspaper as 'a little less than a calamity to the Peterborough poor'. She had provided nursing care to those in the town who might otherwise have received little medical attention, and crowds of grateful people who had benefited from her care lined the streets as her coffin was taken for burial.

Florence Saunders was born in 1856, the daughter of the dean of Peterborough Cathedral. She attended Laurel Court in the minster precincts, the same school that would later educate another girl destined to be a nurse – Edith Cavell. From a young age Florence took it upon herself to visit the poorer areas of the city, trying to bring relief

The home of Florence Saunders, St Oswald's Close.

Before the founding of the National Health Service, improvements in health care often depended on the work of volunteers. Often all that was needed was to educate people about ways they could help themselves. A group of women who wanted to reduce the number of deaths of babies and very young children in Peterborough set up the Fletton Infant Welfare Association in 1915. At the time over fourteen per cent of children died before reaching the age of one. Thanks to their efforts the infant mortality rate fell to three and a half per cent in only one year.

and care to the sick. Many of those still relied on home-made remedies and superstition at times of illness and childbirth. 'Quack medicines' and cure-alls were still readily available even though great advances were being made in medical treatment. Many problems arose from poor housing, overcrowding, and a lack of sanitation and hygiene.

Florence determined to improve the lives of those suffering from illness and the effects of poverty and trained to become a professional nurse at a London hospital. On her return to Peterborough she used her new scientific knowledge to good effect, continuing to visit the sick in their own homes. It is estimated that she made over 100,000 visits in her professional life, travelling from house to house on her tricycle. She founded the Peterborough District Nursing Association in 1884 after undergoing further training.

Her social standing meant that she had access to and influence on local people who were in a position to help her work. Her own home, St Oswald's Close, became the association's headquarters and she employed another nurse to help her. She never took any wages and funded her work herself. Her kindness was legendary – she had a pavilion built in her own garden so that an old lady could live there and receive the treatment she needed. Besides being superintendent of the Peterborough District Nurses' Association, she helped to set up Northamptonshire's County District Nursing Association, becoming its honorary secretary. Nurse Saunders continued her active work of helping the sick right up until her last illness. When she died in 1904, aged only forty-eight, she asked that no monument mark her grave. She left her home to the Nursing Association and when it was sold in 1974, being unsuitable for modern needs, the money from the sale went to continue her charitable works.

Her obituary read:

Notwithstanding the fact that her duties as Superintendent occupied much of her time, Miss Saunders never gave up her active work of visiting, soothing and healing and almost to the last she moved about in the much loved uniform among her humble friends.

AD 1895

STRANGE SIGHTS
IN THE AIR

A Balloon Flight Tragedy and
an 'Out of this World' Visitation

WOMAN PLUNGES TO HER
DEATH FROM BALLOON!

The *Peterborough Advertiser*, 5 August 1895, recorded the tragic death of Mademoiselle Adelaide Bassett as she attempted to parachute from the Victoria 'smoke balloon' on August Bank Holiday, 1895. Crowds came to see the famous Mademoiselle Bassett and her partner Captain Alfred Orton as they performed their dare-devil 'double-aeronaut' parachute jumps. They had successfully completed jumps on at least thirty previous occasions, thrilling spectators as they rose high into the air then parachuted safely to the ground. Some balloonists would hang from a trapeze until they were high enough to jump. The balloon was first tethered over a fire until it filled with smoke and began to rise. Once released, the balloon would soar up, with the two 'aeronauts' seated below harnessed to their parachutes, which would be detached when they leapt from a suitable height. Unfortunately, this type of balloon could easily be blown off course. Although the weather had been wet, the decision was made to go ahead with the show. Affected by the damp air, the heavy canvas balloon did not rise as quickly as it should and the spectators looked on in horror as the tragedy unfolded. The newspaper described the scene:

> What is this? The balloon lurches – it strikes a tree! Then rolls like a huge aerial porpoise against some telegraph wires. Something is wrong! Wires detach Mademoiselle's parachute, it falls and hangs umbrella-like downwards. The crowd get anxious. What does it all mean? The two aloft are seen to confer, and – great horrors – Mademoiselle leaps from her perch, her parachute cannot and will not right itself, and she falls, falls like a wounded bird, 200 feet to the ground, with a sickening thud! A thousand voices exclaim, 'She's killed!'

The fragile frame is shattered to the death and the venturous parachutist five minutes before healthy and full of spirits is now a spine broken corpse in an allotment garden hard by.

At the inquest, Captain Orton explained how he had prevented his colleague from jumping by keeping his arm across her body. When he removed his arm, he shouted, 'For goodness sake Addie, don't go!' Apparently hearing only the word 'Go!', which was her usual signal to jump, she plummeted to her death. Seeing her fall to the ground, Captain Orton did not wait till the balloon had risen higher before jumping himself and rushing to the body of his colleague. The accident caused repercussions well away from Peterborough, as questions were asked in Parliament about the safety record of such stunts, and the death of Mademoiselle Bassett was even recorded in the *Washington Post*. Captain Orton seems to have given up ballooning after the tragic death of his friend.

Hot-air balloons and planes are a common site over the area nowadays but at the beginning of the last century the fascination with flying always drew large crowds and early aviators toured the country giving displays. An air accident with a happier outcome occurred on 12 June 1912. After safely completing a dramatic display of flying at the Milton Golf Course, W.H. Ewen crashed into a tree on take off, fortunately escaping with only minor damage to himself and his plane.

TERROR FROM THE SKIES! THE PETERBOROUGH AIRSHIP SCARE

A strange flying object which beamed bright lights down on the city centre does not seem to have caused mass panic about alien spaceships, but rather worries about a threat from closer at hand.

In the early hours of the morning on 23 March 1909, a Peterborough policeman reported:

I was on duty in Cromwell Road at 5.15 a.m. when I heard what I took to be a motorcar some 400 yards distant. It was quite dark at the time, and I looked along Cromwell Road expecting to see the lights of an approaching car. Nothing appeared, but I could still hear the steady buzz of a high-powered engine. Suddenly it struck me that the sound was coming from above, and I looked up. My eye was at once attracted by a powerful light, which I should judge to have been some 1,200 feet above the ground. I also saw a dark body, oblong and narrow in shape, outlined against the stars. When I first sighted the machine it was not straight overhead but appeared to be over the railway in the direction of Taverners Road. It was travelling at a tremendous pace, and as I watched, the rattle of the engines gradually grew fainter and fainter, until it disappeared in the northwest.

A young lady returning from the theatre also claimed to have seen 'a brilliant flashing light in the sky... apparently

Above   *A Zeppelin under construction. (LC-DIG-ggbain-12237)*

Opposite   *A sketch of the 'dark body' above Peterborough, from a report of the time.*

This portrait, which appeared in the Illustrated London News, *shows Count Zeppelin with the Kaiser.*

attached to some dark object'. Police Constable Kettle was the first person to witness a phenomenon which was reported in different locations throughout East Anglia in the coming months. The German Count Zeppelin had begun to design his airships some years before but it did not seem likely that they were able to cross such distances at that point. However, the strange flying objects gave rise to a fear that the Germans were about to attack England.

WALTER CORNELIUS, BIRDMAN OF PETERBOROUGH

The public's fascination with daring feats, eccentric though they may be, never diminishes. Walter Cornelius, local strongman, earned money for charity by such feats as pushing a double decker bus over half a mile. However, he is best remembered for attempting to fly across the River Nene wearing his homemade wings, drawing great crowds of well-wishers. Every attempt ended as he plunged head first into the water – but at least he was a lifeguard at a local swimming pool!

AD 1890-1910

ELECTION FEVER

'Wild Escapades of the Young Bloods'

ELECTION NIGHTS IN PETERBOROUGH

Reports show that election nights in nineteenth-century Peterborough were wild affairs, seemingly less to do with politics than with battles amongst the townspeople and police.

It became the tradition on election nights for crowds in the Market Square to tear down the hustings (temporary platforms erected for political speeches) and make off with the wood. This led to such riotous behaviour that shops were shut early and boarded up and ladies claimed their places at the upper windows of surrounding buildings to watch the battles. Police threatened those damaging the hustings with prosecution, but to no avail – and things got even more exciting in 1889. Tar barrels were set alight and rolled along the streets as people tried to reach the Angel Hotel on Narrow Bridge Street. The Angel was regarded as Conservative

Party headquarters and eventually a flaming barrel was pushed up onto the hotel steps. As attempts were made to get it through the doors, the landlord rallied guests to throw water onto the barrel and the crowds below, whilst they retaliated by throwing bits of burning wood through the windows.

Drunken mobs went on the rampage again in 1892 and 1895, throwing anything that came to hand at the police who led baton charges to keep them back.

In 1906, supposedly the last great election-night battle took place. The successful candidate was driven in a cab to make speeches at the Liberal club and then set off back to his hotel in town. As the horse had disappeared, the cab was hauled all the way to the Grand Hotel by jubilant supporters. Once they had deposited him there – no tar barrels being available – the cab was filled with straw and set alight, ready for the traditional attempt to reach the Angel (where, presumably, the landlord and guests were arming themselves to fight the fire). Fortunately for all concerned, the blaze was so fierce that the cab burned away completely before it arrived. No mention was made in the local press as to what had happened to the horse!

From then on it seemed that elections and the announcement of the successful candidates were conducted in a more sedate manner. However, this report from a local newspaper in January 1910 would seem to contradict that belief – although the journalist implies things had improved from previous years. Under the headlines 'Wild Escapades of the Young Bloods' and 'smashed windows, traps and heads', the report starts with a description of the huge numbers assembled in Market Square:

> ... such an orderly crowd too, compared with what has been the case at some declarations. Of fun, and good humour and fighting and jostling and horseplay there was plenty, while now and again the nerves of the nervous were startled by what sounded like bombs being exploded in Long Causeway – but they were nothing more than fog signals being laid on the metals of the tram lines and exploded by the passing trams. Squibs and crackers too added to the noise and flare. Collection of tar barrels well-primed, a forest of torches, at least one cab that had been commandeered, filled with hay and saturated with paraffin ready for firing, also a cartload of stones and missiles all deposited at points of vantage ready to be launched upon the crowd.

The Angel Hotel, subject of an arson attempt in 1889.

Not surprisingly, the police 'got wind of the schemes and none came to a head'. Nothing daunted, the crowd were in the mood for more excitement and found their opportunity when a man drove a horse and trap right into the mass of people to hear the speeches made. His bowler hat presented a tempting target and was soon knocked off by people with sticks who began to push and shove the trap, despite being set upon by the driver. Jamming his hat on his head once more, he hit 'a prominent citizen' (who was joining in the fun) in the face with his whip. The journalist seems very pleased to report that the prominent citizen 'returned it with interest by a smashing blow to the man's mouth'. Once the quieter elements of the crowd had gone the rowdier element stayed to sing, dance in the fountains and smash windows, though they apparently did not manage to make use of the various carts laden with hay and soaked in paraffin that were distributed through the rest of the town.

'FEMALE HOOLIGANS'

The Women's Rights Movement engendered strong feelings among many in Peterborough who were opposed to the demand for votes for women. When Emmeline Pankhurst, founder of the Women's Social and Political Union (WSPU), came to speak in Peterborough on 22 February 1911 she received a warm welcome from those who supported her views. However, many would share the opinions quoted in newspapers at the time such as: 'Why not put them in a room, one at a time, say for about an hour with half a dozen mice?' and 'These neurotic women clamour for the vote. What they need is a fire hose.' The *Daily Express'* leader writer even called for suffragette 'criminals' to be transported to St Helena.

In 1913 a hoax bomb was found on the railway line with the message 'Votes for Women: Handle with Care'. Another newspaper reported the reactions of those who believed that suffragettes might target the cathedral:

> They do not want the suffragettes to come, but their spirit is one that says 'by jingo, if they do try their little games on here, there will be trouble for some of them.... Let me catch them', said one of the sentries to an *Express* representative, and although he did not finish the sentence with words, his gesture was expressive.

AD 1860-1912

HORROR, HEARTBREAK AND HUMOUR

The Gruesome Death of 'Clay Pipe Alice'

THE LIFE OF Peterborough woman Alice Mckenzie, also known as Alice Bryant or 'Clay Pipe Alice', ended sometime after midnight on 17 July 1889 in an alley in Whitechapel, East London.

The horrific nature of her injuries, together with the place and date of her death, led to a connection with other murders by the notorious Jack the Ripper. Like earlier victims, Alice Mckenzie was a known prostitute in the Whitechapel area. She liked her drink but preferred smoking – hence her nickname. She had been living with her common-law husband John McCormack for about six years and worked as a washerwoman and cleaner. On the day of her death, she had been given money to pay the rent for their lodgings. However, she had not done so, and appears to have spent the cash on a visit to the music hall and on drink. She was last seen alive rushing towards Whitechapel High Street, close by where her body was discovered lying in a pool of blood, by a policeman in the early hours of the morning. She had been stabbed twice in the neck and it was the severing of an artery that caused her death. Bruises on her body indicated that she had been held down. One knife wound extended from her left breast to her abdomen, though there were smaller cuts on and below her abdomen.

Her injuries were similar to those inflicted on five other women murdered between August and November 1887 by the so-called Jack the Ripper. However, although she had been stabbed in the neck, her throat had not been cut – nor was the mutilation of her body as severe as in the earlier murders. One doctor concluded that the Ripper had killed Alice; the other disagreed. The verdict of the inquest was that she had been killed by 'person or persons unknown'.

SAGE FAMILY OF PETERBOROUGH

Amongst those who perished after the sinking of HMS *Titanic* were eleven members of one Peterborough family. John and Annie Sage were taking their nine children to a new life in Florida when disaster struck.

Leaving his wife to run their baker's and off-licence shop in Gladstone Street, Peterborough, John Sage and his eldest son went to work on the railways in Canada. Hoping to take advantage of the many opportunities to create a better life for his family, he bought land in Florida, intending to start a farm. He and his son returned home to help with the family's move across the Atlantic and booked their passage on the SS *Philadelphia*. Owing to a strike, their tickets for steerage (third class) were transferred to the *Titanic*, about to set out on her maiden voyage. Apparently Annie Sage was apprehensive about the journey because one of her daughters had nearly drowned in the family well. Another story says that she and her eldest daughter had read a novel by Morgan Robertson called *Futility – The Wreck of the* Titan, which increased their anxieties further. *Futility* tells of a great liner, the *Titan*, which struck an iceberg and sank with the loss of most of its passengers – in part due to the lack of lifeboats. Whatever the women's fears, the Sages left Peterborough station for good, waving goodbye to friends and neighbours who had come to see them off. Like so many on board who had dreamt of the new life that awaited them, they would never reach their destination or see their homes again. Not long before midnight on 14 April, when most passengers would have been asleep, the 'unsinkable' liner struck an iceberg and, within less than three hours, sank to the ocean floor. Of the eleven members of the family, only one of their bodies was ever found. They were the largest family group from the *Titanic* to die in the freezing waters of the Atlantic.

Crowd awaiting Titanic *survivors.*

CHARLES DICKENS IN PETERBOROUGH

Dickens seems to have regarded his visits to Peterborough with rather mixed opinions.

Writing to the illustrator Marcus Stone about a reading in Peterborough in October 1859 he is full of praise for his audience:

Charles Dickens, who lectured in Peterborough.

most utterly inert little town in the British dominions.

Perhaps his encounter with the lady who served refreshments at Peterborough Station had upset him. He writes that she had given him 'a cup of tea as if I were a hyena and she my cruel keeper with a strong dislike of me. I ate a petrified bun of enormous antiquity with miserable meekness.' Fortunately, the catering is better these days!

Dickens also visited the Wortley Almshouses in the town before writing *Oliver Twist*. Besides using the buildings as inspiration, he may also have based the character of Mr Bumble on the beadle here.

We had a splendid rush last night – exactly as we supposed, with the pressure on the two shillings, of whom we turned a crowd away. They were a far finer audience than on the previous night; I think the finest I have ever read to.

But other comments are not so complementary:

This is a place which — except the cathedral, with the loveliest front I ever saw — is like the back door to some other place. It is, I should hope, the deadest and

DEATH OF THE CITY'S OLDEST RESIDENT

On 2 April 1830, newspapers recorded the death of Peterborough's oldest inhabitant. Recalling historical events that had occurred over his 200-year lifetime, this resident of the dean's garden had witnessed turbulent times in the city's history. His passing was the cause of great sorrow amongst the citizens of Peterborough – the dean's tortoise is apparently buried in the garden where he spent his life.

AD 1914-1918

THE FIRST WORLD WAR

The Firing Squad, Strange Happenings and an Unlikely Hero

THE OUTBREAK OF the First World War saw the rise of anti-German feeling in the city directed at businesses with German names, even though they had been established in the area for years. Words turned into violence – and one such incident resulted in the reading of the Riot Act for the first and last time in Peterborough.

The Riot Act had been brought in to strengthen the power of magistrates when the behaviour of crowds seriously threatened public order. Once read, groups of twelve or more people had to disperse or risk being arrested. Two local butchers, Franks and Metz, were originally from Germany. Noisy crowds gathered outside Franks's shop, and stones were thrown. As more people joined in and the crowd became more violent, the mayor of Peterborough, Sir Richard Winfrey JP, read the Riot Act over the noise of the mob. In the end about twenty people were fined after damage to these businesses and to the

Salmon and Compass public house. The Franks's own home was also attacked, presumably by those same people who had been happily buying their meat from his shop for years.

Werner, Pfleiderer and Perkins' engineering firm at Westwood was also subjected to accusations of working with the enemy simply because of its name, and in 1915 the company changed the name to Perkins Engineering Ltd.

There was no shortage of local men and boys who were eager to fight for king and country. Even when the horrors of war in the trenches became common knowledge, Peterborough volunteers set off to do their bit. In common with others who joined up en masse from the same place of work or street, the members of the Fletton Victoria Brass Band enlisted together and became part of the Huntingdon Cyclists Battalions during the First World War. After a very short period of training they were sent into action patrolling coastal defences in Yorkshire. Later they were posted to France but no longer operated as a unit.

Those who remained at home rallied round to help the war effort and help those who returned from the Front. The Women's United Total Abstinence Council was formed in 1908 and aimed to turn people away from the evils of drink. They set up a cart selling coffee in the market place to provide an alternative to the pubs. Another welcome initiative was to open a rest room at the railway station for soldiers going to or from the battlefields of the First World War. The women who ran this service originally wanted to create an alternative to alcoholic drink, readily available to workers.

One of the causes of hardship and despair was the abuse of alcohol. Working men had easy access to alcohol in Peterborough's many public houses and a household's weekly income could soon be spent. Some drunkenness led to violence and often a wife would be the first target.

Edith Cavell. (LC-DIG-ggbain-20268)

EDITH CAVELL

Edith Cavell was born on 4 December 1865 in Swardeston, Norfolk, where her father was vicar. She was sent to Laurel Court in the minster precincts at Peterborough as a pupil/teacher. Laurel Court had been founded by Miss Margaret Gibson, a well-respected teacher and local figure who later became the first woman to receive the Freedom of the City. Although seen as a rather eccentric character by some of her pupils, one of whom described her as 'a fearsome dragon', she and her colleague Miss Van Dissell ensured that the girls were well-schooled in languages.

Thanks to Margaret Gibson's connections in Belgium, Edith was offered the job of governess with a family in Brussels. She returned home after five years to nurse her sick father and this experience encouraged her to train as a nurse. In 1907 she returned to Brussels to train nurses at a new clinic and chose to remain in her post when the clinic was taken over as a Red Cross hospital at the outbreak of war.

After the German army took control of Brussels, the British staff members were told to leave, but Edith and her assistant stayed to help both German and Allied soldiers. Believing it was her Christian duty to help others whatever dangers she faced, she hid two British soldiers who made their way to the hospital after becoming stranded behind enemy lines. As a network was set up to repatriate others trying to escape, she continued to help until her actions came to the attention of the German military. Her arrest and interrogation followed, At her trial she did not deny what she had done, though she knew that her confession condemned her. She spent the days before her execution by firing squad preparing quietly for death. In her own words:

> I expected my sentence and I believe it was just. Standing as I do in view of God and Eternity, I realise that patriotism is not enough, I must have no hatred or bitterness towards anyone.

Her re-burial at Norwich Cathedral in 1919 gave honour to the woman who wished to be remembered, not as a war heroine, but as a nurse who tried to do her duty, saving the lives of others.

THOMAS HUNTER – THE LONELY ANZAC

During the First World War, trains carrying wounded soldiers to hospitals around the country often travelled at night, drawing attention away from the numbers of casualties returning from the trenches. One such casualty was Sergeant Thomas Hunter. Originally from Newcastle, Hunter had moved to Australia and joined up there before being sent to Europe. He was so seriously wounded whilst fighting on the Western Front that he was sent back to England to have his injuries treated.

His health deteriorated so much on the journey that the train stopped in Peterborough in order that he could be taken straight to the infirmary in Priestgate (now Peterborough Museum). He died from his wounds in July 1916 and was buried in the town's cemetery. In 1931 the wife of the caretaker of the former hospital claimed that she heard loud footsteps coming up the stairs. Thinking it was her husband returning home, she went out onto the landing to greet him. She was horrified to see the figure of a young man, dressed in green or grey, climb the stairs and turn along the landing through a closed door. More sightings followed and the belief grew up that this was the ghost of poor Thomas Hunter, returning to the scene of his death. Today the museum, formerly the infirmary and before that a private house, claims to be one of the most haunted places in the city.

JIMMY THE DONKEY

Born in June 1916 amidst the horror of the Somme battlefield, Jimmy the donkey ended his days peacefully in Peterborough. Members of the Scottish Rifles adopted him after his mother was killed and made him their mascot. He apparently learned to 'salute' by lifting a front leg and knew how to beg for titbits as he carried ammunition around the trenches. Despite being wounded seven times, Jimmy survived the war and was brought back to England. The Peterborough branch of the RSPCA bought him and he became well-known in the town, especially popular with children, as he raised money for the RSPCA. When he died in 1943, the donkey was buried in the town's Central Park. A memorial service was held for Jimmy and the stone restored in 2003.

The French Red Cross at the Somme, where terrible conditions prevailed. Jimmy the Donkey was born during the battle. (LC-DIG-npcc-31144)

WAR AGAIN

Airfields and Special Forces

PETERBOROUGH WAS WELL-PREPARED when war was declared in 1939.

Public air-raid shelters appeared in various locations around the city, street lighting was altered and white lines were painted along roads and around lamp posts and other roadside structures.

The public bathhouse behind Peterborough Museum was brought into use as the town prepared to deal with the threat of poison gas attacks. In the event of an attack, people who had been exposed to the gas had to make their way to the new decontamination unit. Once there, they had to take off their clothes for burning and wash thoroughly to limit damage to their skin. The signs directing people for decontamination remain today.

Food rationing began and an army of volunteers came forward to work for the war effort. People queued up to enlist before compulsory call-up was introduced. So soon after the 'war to end

all wars', families again said goodbye to their loved ones, many never to return. The memorials and remembrance books of all who lost their lives are to be found in the tiny, peaceful chapel of St Sprite inside the beauty of the cathedral.

Evacuees began to arrive from London and local schools had to change lesson times to cater for the huge increase in student numbers. Peterborough had been chosen as a safe haven for evacuees coming from areas likely to suffer heavy bombing raids. A town where the engineering industry turned to wartime

Opposite   *Sign for decontamination.*

Right   *Poster from 1918 reflecting the anti-Germanic feeling that sparked riots in Peterborough: 'Once a German, always a German!'*

production and where there were major railway marshalling yards might not have been the obvious choice, especially as Peterborough was surrounded by air bases and had a pilot training base at Westwood. Generally, though, the area escaped the damage suffered by some cities. During 1941 a railway worker died during an attack on the New England marshalling yards and two fire watchers died in Priestgate in the city centre.

The first air raid in 1940 damaged shops and the Lido swimming pool. There were civilian casualties after raids during the course of the war when houses were damaged.

On 10 June 1942 over 200 incendiary bombs landed on buildings in the town centre, including the cathedral and Town Hall. Thanks to the quick work of the ARP (Air Raid Precautions) wardens and fire watchers, damage was limited. Fire watchers would scan the skies for signs of enemy aircraft and were provided with a stirrup pump to access water supplies, a bucket of sand and a bucket of water.

Even the local Symington's factory, which manufactured ladies' undergarments and corsets, turned to war work. Symington's had long been a major employer of women and the workforce began to produce parachutes. Later, families who had been involved in the factory's war effort were offered parachute silk. Most people were pleased to have the opportunity to make extra clothes and eke out their clothing rations, though others were none too happy with the colours they were given!

The flat countryside around Peterborough made it an ideal location for air bases. A 'dummy' airfield was constructed at Maxey to fool German planes into dropping their bombs away from actual RAF bases. RAF Wittering had been established during the First World War as a base for anti-Zeppelin fighters, and during the Second World War it was used by fighter planes. The airfield was bombed five times and on one occasion seventeen men died. Heavy bombers flew from RAF Polebrook, which later became a base for the United States Air Force.

Clarke Gable came to Polebrook to make a recruiting film for gunners and flew several missions from the base. He often visited pubs in Peterborough, including the Blue Peter. The American Services' Club was in Peterscourt, a former teacher training college that was designed by George Gilbert Scott, the architect of St Pancras Station and the Albert Memorial in London. A reminder of the Second World War is the doorway at the side of the building, rescued from the London Guildhall during the London Blitz and brought to his offices in Peterscourt by Frank Perkins, founder of the Perkins Engines Co.

THE JEDBURGHS – THE SECRET ARMY

Milton Hall near Peterborough, the private residence of the Fitzwilliam family from the sixteenth century, was used as training base by a Special Operations Unit during the Second World War. The Jedburghs were drawn from several nationalities and were trained to operate behind enemy lines. Small teams were parachuted into enemy territory to supply expertise and arms to the local resistance. The bravery of these volunteers meant that the work of the resistance could be co-ordinated with the Allies' plans, leading to more effective communication and acts of sabotage. A memorial to those who died during the course of the war is located in the St Sprite's chapel of Peterborough Cathedral.

UP TO DATE

FIRE!

Nearly the End for Peterborough's Magnificent Cathedral

THERE HAVE BEEN many fires over the centuries that have caused great damage to the centre of town. As most of the houses were mainly built out of wood, fires spread quickly and caused great damage. In later times, fines were levied on landlords who had no chimneys on their property – trouble obviously waiting to happen! There was no organised group to tackle a blaze, so people had to rely on volunteers to give what help they could. On one occasion a wine merchant supplied barrels – presumably empty – from his cellar to help carry water to the flames! Buckets were kept in St John's church ready for use in an emergency and would be filled at the nearest well. In the sixteenth and seventeenth centuries two major fires burnt out large areas of Westgate and Bridge Street. Water pumps had to be operated by hand and the men who worked them were paid in beer. The temptation was too much for one man, who started fires deliberately in antici-pation of a free drink – though unfortunately he was found out, and hanged. A fire in 1834 destroyed thirty-five houses in Westgate, though only one person died.

An official fire service was set up in 1844 but with no access to a good pumped water supply their job was not easy. They were not able to deal with big emergencies such as the fire which broke out at the infirmary in 1884. Patients had to be evacuated, and though none lost their life the potential for tragedy served to highlight the need for more effective measures in future. A group of local businessmen met at the Angel Hotel to discuss what to do, with the result that the Peterborough Volunteer Fire Service was formed. They did not have to wait long to go into action, as a fire broke out at the Phoenix Brewery in Priestgate, opposite the infirmary. The Peterborough Volunteer Fire Service is the only one of its kind still operating in the country today. Its members receive no pay for their excellent work and were awarded the Freedom of the City in 1984.

An early nineteenth-century fire crew in action.

In more recent times there have been two city centre blazes which involved not only the local fire brigades but others from around the area. In August 1956 a passer-by spotted a fire in the window of the Robert Sayle's store in Cowgate. Flames well over a 100ft high engulfed the four-storey building and spread to premises nearby, including the other Robert Sayle building in the city centre. Over 100 firemen were unable to stop the destruction of the store or of some of the neighbouring businesses. Two firemen had to be treated in hospital but otherwise there were no casualties.

The abbey church had risen from the ashes on at least two earlier occasions in its long history, but on the 22 November 2001 the cathedral could have suffered the fate of earlier buildings on the site. As the verger was walking through the darkened minster precincts that November evening after the last service of the day, he noticed a flickering light through the windows. After the alarm was raised, the first fear was that the great painted wooden ceiling would be destroyed and that the roof would collapse. When firemen entered the building they saw that the flames had not reached the ceiling but had a difficult job ahead of them to put out the fire without causing more damage to the interior as they did so.

Next morning, relief that an even greater disaster had been averted was tempered with the enormity of the task that lay ahead. Cleaning and conservation work on the ceiling, the oldest and largest painted wooden ceiling in Europe, was almost complete after nearly five years. The whole process had to begin again. Arson was suspected after the source of the fire was traced to a candle left in the middle of a pile of plastic chairs. The whole interior was blackened with soot, the organ had been damaged both by fire and by water and some of the windows had cracked. A massive cleaning operation began and the people of Peterborough rallied round to raise money and to offer help so that the cathedral could be restored to its former light and glory.

CONCLUSION

THE TWENTY-FIRST CENTURY sees Peterborough as a growing commercial centre, still attracting newcomers from many countries. The visible signs of industry have gone from the city centre but the farmlands and countryside are not far away. Cathedral (formerly Market) Square, with all its new shops and cafés, is still dominated by the cathedral. St John's church sits in the centre of the square surrounded by open spaces, benches and fountains.

The main road from the cathedral precincts is closed to vehicles and people walk along it to the river as they did when the first monks began to build their church. Steam trains run along the river bank from Wansford but these days the trains of the Nene Valley Railway are for pleasure trips only. Boats passing along the Nene through the town no longer carry stone or grain for the brewing industry.

However busy and noisy the city is, you can walk through the original heavy wooden gates in the Norman Archway and find peace in the minster precincts. A far cry from the days when the abbey and town were at loggerheads and violence was not far away. People are now welcomed into the church behind the walls and it takes a great leap of the imagination to picture the destruction that was wrought in this place. Whatever has happened in the past, who knows what stories will be passed on about our city in the future?

If you enjoyed this book, you may also be interested in…

Haunted Peterborough
STUART ORME

Peterborough has a rich and fascinating history, stretching back 3,500 years to the Bronze Age. The city is a vibrant place with a new town surrounding an ancient town centre, still dominated by its Norman cathedral. But the city has a sinister and spooky side… Written by the creator and guide of the city's popular ghost walks, discover the spooky side of Peterborough's past. Uncover the eerie secrets of the city, from apparitions of monks to ghostly children, a slaughtered Cavalier and the ghosts of the cathedral prencints…

978 07524 7654 4

Cambridgeshire: Strange but True
ROBERT HALLIDAY

This volume (which includes the old county of Huntingdonshire and the city of Peterborough) illustrates unusual, odd and extraordinary people, places and incidents. Discover the origin of the expression 'Hobson's Choice', a woman who survived nine days trapped in a snow cave, the floating church of the Fens, and many more tales on university life, local characters, historic buildings, and strange customs and traditions.

978 07509 4059 7

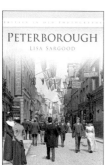

Britain in Old Photographs: Peterborough
LISA SARGOOD

This book brings to light a fascinating collection of images from the city's museum archives and library files. Some of the views are of streets and buildings which are instantly recognisable, but others show scenes that have long since disappeared, been demolished or altered beyond recognition. These pictures are priceless, capturing moments in Peterborough's history that would otherwise be lost forever.

978 07524 5434 4

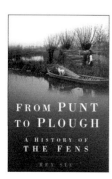

From Punt to Plough: A History of the Fens
REX SLY

The Fens are the largest plain in the British Isles, covering an area of nearly three-quarters of a million acres. Fen people know the area as marsh (land reclaimed from the sea) and fen (land drained from flooding rivers running from the uplands). The Fens are unique in having more miles of navigable waterways than anywhere else in Britain. Rex Sly's new book draws on his many years of research, and his knowledge of and love of the Fens shines through on every page.

978 07509 3398 8

Visit our website and discover thousands of other History Press books.

www.thehistorypress.co.uk